Ins

Karl Barth's Reflections on the Life of Faith

Karl Barth

SELECTED BY
Eberhard Busch

TRANSLATED BY
O. C. Dean Jr.

WJK WESTMINSTER
JOHN KNOX PRESS
LOUISVILLE · KENTUCKY

© 2009 Westminster John Knox Press

Translated by O. C. Dean Jr. from the German *Augenblicke* published
by Theologischer Verlag Zürich, Zurich, Switzerland
© 2001 by Theologischer Verlag Zürich, Zurich, Switzerland

First English edition
Westminster John Knox Press
Louisville, Kentucky

09 10 11 12 13 14 15 16 17 18—10 9 8 7 6 5 4 3 2 1

Book design by Sharon Adams
Cover design by Lisa Buckley

Library of Congress Cataloging-in-Publication Data

Barth, Karl, 1886–1968.
  [Augenblicke. English]
  Insights : Karl Barth's reflections on the life of faith / Karl Barth ; selected
by Eberhard Busch ; translated by O. C. Dean Jr.—1st ed.
    p. cm.
  Includes bibliographical references.
  ISBN 978-0-664-23239-9 (alk. paper)
  1. Meditations.   I. Busch, Eberhard, 1937–   II. Title.
  BV4834.B3313   2009
  242—dc22   2008030390

Contents

Foreword

Insights.

Insights for looking within oneself or for looking beyond. Insights for taking a deep breath, for reflecting, for being amazed, for smiling, for questioning. Insights for looking upward and for stepping forward, for gathering courage and for being content . . . Karl Barth invites and stimulates such insights. He lived from 1886 to 1968; he was a Swiss pastor for twelve years and a theology professor for over forty years: fifteen years in Germany and twenty-five years in his hometown of Basel, Switzerland.

One of Barth's most beautiful sermons, preached in the Basel prison on his seventieth birthday, interprets Psalm 34:5 in this way: "Look to him, and have a radiant countenance." And in his gigantic *Church Dogmatics* (*Die Kirchliche Dogmatik* appeared in thirteen parts between 1932 and 1967) he calls that the "root formation of all humanity": the great, solemn, incomparable moment "when between two people there is an 'insight,' that is, when they look into each other's eyes and discover each other." When we think in this way, we can speak of "insights," moments that do not pass by empty, but are filled—seriously, cheerfully, comfortingly, reflectively—with the countenance of God and of our fellow creatures.

In the present volume Karl Barth's texts (in his own characteristic way of writing) have been gathered from his rich output and arranged in a delightfully colorful bouquet. Some are self-contained short selections; others comprise fragments of thought from various sources, all of which are listed at the end. In each case the text is preceded by a Bible quotation either derived from the text itself or supplied by the editor. They point to the light in which Barth saw human life and in the same way in which he saw it. Perhaps these texts will serve as greetings that promise the reader a good time.

Eberhard Busch

Translator's Preface

As was the practice of his day, Karl Barth wrote in a language that was male oriented and dominated by masculine nouns, for example, for "God" and "human being." This language has, for the most part, been updated in accordance with the practices of the New Revised Standard Version of the Bible (NRSV); that is, most references to human beings have become gender-inclusive, whereas references to the Deity have remained masculine.

While scriptural quotations are mostly from the NRSV, it was necessary at times to substitute the King James Version (KJV), the Revised Standard Version (RSV), or a literal translation of the Luther version quoted or paraphrased by Barth, in order to allow the author to make his point.

O. C. Dean Jr.

Confident Courage

Amazement

They will be amazed by all of the good.
(Jer. 33:9, Luther)

At the beginning of all theological perception, research, and thought—and also of every theological statement—stands a quite specific amazement. Its lack in even the best theologian will threaten the heart of the entire enterprise, while even bad theologians are not a lost cause in their service and their duty, as long as they are still capable of amazement. Amazement occurs when we happen upon a spiritual or natural phenomenon that we have not yet encountered, that we are not used to, that is initially unfamiliar, strange, and new. It is a phenomenon that we do not know how to begin to integrate into the realm of what we believe to be possible, and about its origin and essence we can only ask, until further information is available.

The amazement that overcomes us when we get involved with theology, however, is of a different kind. To be sure, it also brings astonishment and forces us to learn, but in this case there can be no talk of one day learning all there is to know, of the unusual ever seeming usual and the new becoming old hat, of the foreign ever becoming domesticated. Here, progress in study can only mean that the stopping short and questioning in regard to the object of study will increase, and far from ever in some sense letting us go, this amazement will more and more gain the upper hand. If we ever really experience this amazement, we will become, once and for all time, totally amazed human beings.

Great God

"My soul magnifies the Lord."
(Luke 1:47)

God wants to be magnified, made great, in our miserable human lives. What does this "magnification" of God mean? It is something simple and yet everlasting, something only to be known as a miracle. It means, namely, that in our little existence, in the days and years and decades in which our life is given to us, in the cares and problems and struggles of our life, we are called again and again, step by step, to let God be the Lord.

Why? Because God is God! Not for any other reason. Not because we think it is useful, but simply because God is the Lord. To let God himself be the Lord, to let him reign in our thoughts, in our heart and soul, in our conscience, means a very simple relationship: God is God the Lord, and as such he now wants to reign in my life, and I can let him reign as Lord only in each step of my life—whether large or small—and that would mean to magnify God. That would mean: "My soul magnifies the Lord"!

Then with us God would also be what he is in himself. That is his grace: that it is not too small a thing for him to be your God and my God, and therefore also to be magnified by us.

Comforting Laughter

Look to him, and have a radiant countenance.
(Barth, after Ps. 34:5)

When we look to him, to Jesus Christ, then we experience a transformation beside which the greatest revolution is a small affair. It simply consists in the fact that whoever looks to him and believes in him can be called and can be a child of God here on earth. This is an inner transformation, however, that cannot be and remain merely internal, but rather takes place by pushing powerfully toward the outside. A great, bright, lasting light comes on. And this very light finds its reflection in believers' faces, in their eyes, in their behavior, in their words and actions. Such people—in the very midst of their troubles and suffering, and contrary to all their sighing and grumbling—know joy: not a cheap and superficial joy but a deep joy; not a passing but an abiding joy. And even if they may still seem to others to remain sad and in a bad way, joy turns them into people who are basically happy. We may rest assured that they have received something to laugh about and cannot hold back this laughter even if otherwise they have nothing to laugh about. It is not evil laughter but good laughter, not scornful but kind and comforting; nor is it diplomatic laughter, as has become usual in politics, but sincere laughter that comes from deep down in one's heart.

Humor

"For you will laugh."
(Luke 6:21)

Having a sense of humor means not being stiff but flexible. Humor arises when we have insight into the contradiction between our existence as children of God and as children of this age, and we become conscious of our actions in a lively way. Humor means a great bracketing of the serious side of the present. There is humor only in our struggle with the serious side of the present. But we, as children of God, cannot possibly remain entirely serious about and in this struggle. God's future makes itself known as that smile under tears, as that joyfulness in which we can bear the present and take things seriously within the bracket, because the present already carries the future within it. This is also what distinguishes genuine humor from the false: that it presupposes knowledge of suffering, and also, quite clearly, that it prefers not to be practiced on others but on oneself: that one sees the bracket in which one finds oneself. Therefore, it then will become something that will relieve and liberate—and not poison and gall—when it is directed against others. Those who laugh at themselves are also allowed to laugh at others and will joyfully also pass the ultimate test of being laughed at themselves—a test that much alleged humor usually fails miserably.

Upheld

Then Peter began to sink, but Jesus caught him.
(cf. Matt. 14:30–31)

The fact that Peter is sinking does not mean that Jesus Christ is also sinking. And as long as Jesus does not sink, Peter cannot completely sink either, if he remembers only one thing: that he must now rely totally on Jesus. Indeed, even if Christians fail—even if God's outstanding members fail—they still remain those who are called. This remains their service, and it remains their commission. The greatest servants of God have disgraced God. But God has not therefore abandoned them and theirs. When we are unfaithful, God is faithful, and only one thing is required: that we think about it, and when we no longer know how to help ourselves, we cry to God from our hearts and say: Lord, help me! Because there is this calling from out of the depths, which in reality only means the mercifulness of God; then it's just a matter of making use of it. Now it is a question of drawing back from hurrying into waiting, in order to be strengthened for new tasks. For there is no question that Jesus Christ lets his own become weak, so that they may be made all the stronger. "Jesus caught him." This catching is the most marvelous strengthening that can be imagined. As such it is always for the weak. And these weak are then stronger than the strongest of this world. If we can only learn to put our confidence in one thing: You are truly God's Son. You, our Savior. You!

Under Care

"I will give you rest."
(Matt. 11:28)

These who have rest are not the ones who have no unrest. Those who have rest are not the ones who are lazy and self-centered enough to cause themselves no unrest or to keep unrest away from their bodies. Suppressed unrest is not rest. Those who have rest are the ones who in the midst of unrest know themselves to be under care, who—even when they certainly will not fail to take care—do not mean that they have to take themselves under care, but rather know that they have been taken under care. And those who have rest are the ones who in all unrest know themselves to be free. Those who are free see and even tolerate the walls that surround them on all sides, but they also see how these barriers are penetrated by windows and doors. And what greets them there from the other side is the free world of God, which they are approaching and which they can live in even today. For even today they can see how small and transitory their prison is and how large and eternal this world of God is. And those who have rest are the ones who know themselves bound in the middle of unrest, bound to his place, to his way in this life, as it is now allotted to them. They have rest who know something higher than their own cravings and their own arbitrary use of power, higher than all those strange ideas that daily fall on their ears, and higher than the blind coincidences that drive them this way and that. Who of us has rest in this sense? Jesus says, "I will give you rest."

Rest

And the LORD gave them rest on every side.
(Josh. 21:44)

We do not find rest through all kinds of experiments. We cannot chase after it with all kinds of knowledge about life and the art of living, with all kinds of psychology and astrology, with all kinds of education and self-education, with all of this beautiful stuff that we love so much. With all of that we can get only a small idea of what it would be like if we had rest. All of that we can also use, and may well do so, when we have already found rest—just as children who have been brought to their place may play and will play with usefulness and advantage. What is not possible, however, is that with all of that we can obtain rest for ourselves. Why not? Because we quite simply must know God in order to know ourselves protected in unrest—that is, in order to have rest. But we can know about God only through God. We have to learn about God through God himself. Only through God himself can we be granted forgiveness of our sins and eternal life. We must experience God coming down to our level. In short, Jesus must give us rest. And that is just what he says to us. That is the one thing that we may hear from him: "I will give you rest." That is what we may hear from him who is the "coming down" of God. What he gives is rest. And those to whom he gives what he has to give will have rest.

Contentment

The LORD is my shepherd, I shall not want.
(Ps. 23:1)

Those who have God really have everything—hardly as they would like to have it, but all the more certainly as God wants them to have everything, so that they can be content. Let them be content with God alone. Human beings have no glory of their own that would allow them to be content. Human beings are not self-sufficient. Therefore there is no way that they can be self-content. Just as surely, they are only human beings and not God, and indeed are in contradiction to God! But in all things— and threatened by all things—we see the glory of God and are effectively and finally comforted in all of these threats. And this state of being comforted by the glory of God is true contentment. For this is the very glory of God: that God does not keep the fullness of his divine being for himself, but communicates and demonstrates that he wants to find his own contentment in being our Shepherd. When that is seen and heard, the answer can only be: "I shall not want"! Any want could only consist in our closing ourselves off from the glory of God and thus in our resistance against the shepherding of God. For the glory of God is the love of God. Why is it that here we are resistant and rebellious? As certainly as the Lord is my shepherd, I shall want for nothing, and that means that I do not have to be resistant and rebellious.

Unworried

"Do not worry."
(Matt. 6:25)

We cannot believe and worry. Or, rather, when we believe, we can only believe and in this faith cast all our worries on the Lord. If we act otherwise, then we just don't believe, and then, of course, we are lost. Then things don't work in the practical world, either. Then we also fail in reality. Then we no longer find anything to hold on to. Then we no longer know how to help ourselves. Then the long discussions begin again, and the little embarrassments. Once again we are what we were when we started out, and the inward and outward strength of the Lord is gone again. We are again petty little human beings, a little bit too bold, a little bit too impractical in the way we tackle things. And then? Well, then it's over. The misfortune in the church consists simply in the fact that people have always believed too little. Oh, they have always believed so strongly and so boldly! But the misfortune was always that in believing they have then still looked at the other side, where the focus is no longer on Jesus but on tactical and practical matters, on one's own self and its wishes and its embarrassment, on people, on the course of the world. If they had only believed, then they would not even have needed to believe so boldly. A mustard seed would have had the power to move mountains.

Fearless

"Have no fear."
(Matt. 10:26)

What should we do, then, so that the nations will really want peace? First of all, we should not have so much fear—namely, about the evil intentions of others. Naturally, anyone can be anxious in today's world. But we can do many things that are precisely what we should not do. If we don't act as if our dear God is dying, and as if others are planning to eat us in the near future, then we will be doing our part for world peace. Second, those who do not want to be afraid must be people who have decided to see with their own eyes, to hear with their own ears, and to think with their own heads. They must not let themselves be turned into a mass product through public opinion or propaganda. Peace is in danger because there are so few free people. And, third, people who have no fear are those who are fully open to the troubles and needs of their fellow human beings and to the question of how they can be of assistance, but who, by contrast, are capable of not taking themselves and their own ideas so terribly seriously. The danger of war is also always present when so many people have swallowed some kind of yardstick. Away with the yardsticks! Those who cannot sigh with others and laugh a little bit about themselves are warmongers. One more thing: a great fear of God is required if one really wants to have peace.

Joy in God

"My spirit rejoices in God my Savior."
(Luke 1:47)

When we speak of the work of God, we do not mean an ultimate eerie power that we feel somehow and somewhere, nor do we mean the fate that like an iron ring holds the world together, nor one of those ideas in which we summarize what for us is the greatest value, the best, or the highest, what is beauty, what is truth. We cannot say of any of these gods: "My spirit rejoices in you." We can rejoice only in the one whom we call "God my Savior"—that is, the one who has come to help us and who already tells us with his presence that we are in need of help. However it may be with everything else, he is the one who helps us, who accepts us, who brings us holiness in the midst of our unholy existence. That is God the Savior, and in this God we may and can and must rejoice. About the other gods one may reflect, may bow to fate with a dark face, and with self-made comfort may pursue their ideas fanatically. But where is the joy in that? Joy is the rarest and most infrequent thing in the world. We already have enough fanatical seriousness, enthusiasm, and humorless zeal in the world. But joy? This shows us that the perception of the living God is rare. When we have found God our Savior—or when he has found us—we will rejoice in him.

Thank God!

Bless the LORD, O my soul.
(Ps. 103:1)

Among Christians there are far too many grouchy and sour faces. You have no reason to look that way, and it does you no good. You are a work of God. He has created you and done so much for you that is good. And now your task consists simply in your being the one created by him and endowed by him. So, now be the one endowed by him, and since you are that one, don't fail to sing God's praise, even if you have no imposing voice. Don't fail to live in the joy in which you have been placed, even if you can only make that joy imperfectly apparent. That is not an art. You can do it too. May God the Father, the Son, and the Holy Spirit prevail and make this happen among us human beings!

O Lord, our God, we have no praise to offer that is worthy of you, if you do not lay it upon our hearts and lips, if you do not want to turn our whole lives and all our thoughts, words, and works into your praise and accept them as your praise. We pray to you that you will want to do that. And for all of Christendom on earth we ask you that it may be given the power to praise you better, more sincerely, more strongly than before. We pray to you that you would bring about new praise in the whole confused, divided, tormented humanity of our day. None of us has any other helper but you. Amen.

The Living God

God Is Alive

My soul thirsts . . . for the living God.
(Ps. 42:2)

That is a living God: a God who is really God. Not a fifth wheel on the wagon, but the wheel that drives all the wheels. Not a sacred relic set apart, but someone who steps with power into the middle of everything that is. Not a dark power in the clouds beside which human beings can only be slaves or that they avoid like willful schoolboys escaping a pedantic teacher, but the clear power of freedom that is over all and in all and that would like to be honored first in humankind. Not an idea, not a view, but the living power that overcomes the powers of death, as real as the power of electricity or the force of dynamite! Not a decoration of the world, but a lever that reaches into the earth. Not a feeling with which one plays, but a fact that one takes seriously, on which one can stand with both feet in every situation, on which one feeds like bread, into which one retreats as into a fortress, from which one breaks out like people under assault who venture one happy sally after another on all sides. That means a living God. Are you astonished that something like that should be possible? Then, there will be still much more to be astonished about. Now we have only a dim perception of him, the living God. There can be no talk of knowing him, of "having" him. What awkward sighing and stammering there is, when we try to say something about him!

God in the Highest

"Glory to God in the highest."
(Luke 2:14, RSV)

In distinction to all other gods, the God of the Christian confession of faith is not an invented god, not a finite god ultimately discovered by human beings. He is not the fulfillment of what humankind was in the process of seeking and finding. Rather, we Christians speak of the One who simply takes the place of what is normally meant by the word "god" and thus drives out everything else and alone claims to be truth. When the true God appears, the gods bite the dust, and God remains the only God. He is the one who stands over us and also over our highest and lowest feelings, strivings, and intuitions, and over the products of the human spirit, even if these products are the most sublime. And this also means that God is not only unprovable and unsearchable, but also incomprehensible. "God in the highest" means the one who simply is founded in himself and thus really is, and who can be and is revealed to us again and again only through himself. This very God in the highest has, as such, turned to humankind. "God in the highest" does not mean a wholly other who has nothing to do with us; rather, it means the one who from out of the highest has come down to us. God in the highest is the God who proves himself to be really God and thus the one who in no way is in our hands, but who nonetheless—and in this very way—has looked after us.

God's Power

"For thine. . . is the power."
(Matt. 6:13, KJV)

The power of God is distinct from any powerlessness. There is also a power of powerlessness. But God is neither entirely nor partially powerless. He is different from all other powers in that he can do what he wants to do. God is superior to all other powers. These other powers impose themselves upon us in a way that is different from God. God is not in a series of these worldly powers as, say, the highest of them; he is not limited or conditioned by them. He is the Lord of all lords. And God is not "power in itself." Who God is cannot be understood as the highest epitome of power. And those who call the "almighty one" God are missing God in the most frightful way. For the "almighty one" is the Devil. Where power wants to be its own authority and determine justice, we are dealing with the "revolution of nihilism." Power in itself is evil. The power of God is set over against this power in itself. The power of God is from the start the power of justice. It is power based on justice. The omnipotence of God as the power of justice is the power of God that in itself is love. Whatever works against this love is injustice and therefore not really power. God's power is genuine power. This power is the power of his free love in Jesus Christ, which is confirmed and revealed in him.

God's Election

[Jesus said,] "I chose you."
(John 15:16)

It is really God's grace, goodwill, and favor that his creatures experience in such a way that the mystery of their divine election so movingly permeates their lives. When that happens, God is really saying yes to them. And this is a yes that is unconditional in its certainty and precedes all self-determination of the creatures: the foreordination under which they may live in all circumstances. It sets us in motion, but it does not throw us into unrest. The realm of unrest is the region outside of the divine election of grace, the realm of creatures who resist the love of God. They must be restless, for they have let themselves fall into this resistance and now, after they have let go of their only possible security, are searching in vain for another one. But through God's election of grace, his creatures are snatched away from this realm of unrest. When God says yes to them, yes is said to them: no ifs or buts, no ulterior motives or reservations, not in temporal but in eternal faithfulness. The question whether this yes could be valid or not, the worry of how one could get hold of and keep this yes, the despair when faced with the repeatedly emerging impossibility of living by this yes on one's own—all of that lies behind God's creatures, because God's election has already taken place. They are affirmed; they no longer have any other way of living than by this yes, as surely as God has said this yes and as surely as God is God. All that is left for them is calmly to live the life that has been thus defined. They are left with only the wonder, the reverent astonishment, in the face of the fact of the mystery that they may live this affirmed life.

God's Faithfulness

The gifts and the calling of God are irrevocable.
(Rom. 11:29)

The fact that in the year 70 the Jews did not disappear from world history, but of all the larger and smaller peoples in their ancient environment, precisely they continued to exist and continue to exist today more energetically than ever, is based clearly—from the perspective of the biblical message—on the idea that God's decision in the election of precisely this people and in his covenanting precisely with them is an eternal, immovable decision. The fact that this people was an unfaithful people that always wanted to be a nation and have a king and have a history like other nations—none of that can change God's faithfulness. Because the election and the covenant survive—not abolished but fulfilled in Jesus Christ—the Jews also survive in the history of the world, the people who are not a nation and yet in this very way are the people who are God's people, with a history that is not a history and yet in this very way, in its world-historical problematic, is the truly human history, the history of humankind with God. Because the Jews are these things, it is true of them even to this day: "Truly, one who touches you touches the apple of my eye" (Zech. 2:8). But no one can touch God's eye.

God's Humanity

The . . . loving kindness of God . . . appeared.
(Titus 3:4)

God does not need to be nonhuman in order to be truly God. It would be a false god's false divinity in and with which we did not also immediately meet with his humanity. Such false divinities are mocked once and for all time in Jesus Christ. In him it was decided once and for all time that God does not exist without humankind. It's not as if God needs human beings in order to be truly God as their partner. He does not have to be *for* human beings; one might think, rather, that he has to be *against* human beings. But that is the mystery in which he meets us in the existence of Jesus Christ: in his freedom he wants to be not against human beings but for them—he wants, in fact, to be the partner of human beings and their almighty, compassionate savior. Is it not true that in Jesus Christ, as he is attested to us in the Holy Scripture, precisely in himself, genuine divinity, as well as genuine humanity, is incorporated? Indeed, there is the father who has compassion on his lost son, the king on his destitute debtor, the Samaritan on the man who had fallen among thieves. If Jesus Christ is the word of truth, the "mirror of the fatherly heart of God" (Luther), then Nietzsche's statement that humanity is something that must be overcome is a barefaced lie. Then the truth of God is to be found precisely here and nowhere else: in his benevolence toward humanity.

God's Compasssion

Jesus . . . said, "I have compassion for the crowd."
(Matt. 15:32)

The expression is much stronger than the translation suggests. The expression means: the need and the suffering, the wrongfulness and the helplessness, the abandonment and endangerment of these people affect Jesus, not only mentally but also in his heart, in his very being. He took it from them and onto himself; he let it be his own misery; he bore it and endured it in their place. And in this very act, he became and was for them far more than one who looked at their work and fate in mere sympathy, and also more than a preacher, pastor, comforter, and admonisher. For them he became and was their helper and rescuer, the creator of a new situation, a new existence. And all of this because he had compassion for them. Compassion is the behavior in which someone steps in for another person who is in need, someone who is there for and acts for that other person. Jesus is the one who in this sense had compassion. That is his humanity. He fulfills the will of God by being there for human beings, by dying for them, in order to live for them. Therefore, Jesus is for us human beings, because God himself is for us. And God himself is for us, in that the human being Jesus is for us. Reflected in the humanity of Jesus is the nature of God himself. Being together and being powerfully for each other are first and originally in him, the triune God himself. God not only loves but is love. And as eternal love he himself is active in the world and proclaims himself in the humanity of Jesus.

The Neighbor

The Burden Bearer

"Here is the Lamb of God who takes away the sin of the world!"

(John 1:29)

That is what happened in what he—as the Son of God and the One sent by God and in God's name—did and still does for the world, for its reconciliation with God, and for each one of us, for our salvation. He did and does this as the great, the incomparable, the only true burden bearer of his kind. That happened when all the sins, all the trespasses, all the transgressions, all the aberrations, all the wrongs of the whole world, of all times and lands—including our own—were loaded onto him, as if he had made himself guilty of them all. That happened when he did not complain in the face of this sea of horrors and did not rebel against such an outrageous imposition, but took this entire load upon himself willingly, let our sin be his sin, our misery be his misery. That happened when he bore this entire burden: "He himself bore our sins in his body on the cross" (1 Pet. 2:24). It happened when he took the burden away, abolished it, wiped it out, and liberated all of us from it, by dying on the cross. That is what happened, but more than that happened. As the great burden bearer and thus as the fulfiller of almighty love, he rose from the dead, lives, shines, and rules now and forever in eternity. Not as a powerful conqueror but as the great burden bearer, he has made the world his kingdom and property, and called all of us as members of this kingdom. As our liberator he became and is our lawgiver. And there is just one thing that his law wants of us: that we who have been liberated by the great burden bearer might be able to live through him.

Christmas

And she . . . laid him in a manger.
(Luke 2:7)

The Savior no longer needs to be born. He was born once and for all time. But he would like to come stay with us. The place where the Savior would like to come stay with us has in common with the stall of Bethlehem that it too is not at all beautiful but looks rather desolate, not at all cozy but downright sinister, not worthy of human beings but quite close to the animals. Our inns, proud or modest, and we as their residents—that is only the surface of our life. Hidden underneath there is a depth, a bottom—indeed, an abyss. And there below are we human beings, each in our way, only poor beggars, only lost sinners, only sighing and dying creatures, only people who are now at their wit's end. And at this very time Jesus Christ comes to stay with us, and what's more: he has already come to stay with us. Yes, thanks be to God for this dark place, for this manger, for this stall also in our life! There below we need him, and even there he can also need us, each one of us. There we are just the right ones. There he only waits for us to see him, to know him, to believe in him, to love him. There he greets us. There we can do nothing other than greet him again and bid him welcome. Let us not be ashamed to be down there right beside the ox and the ass! Right there is where he holds fast to us all.

Good Friday

At three o'clock Jesus cried out . . .
"My God, my God, why have you forsaken me?"
(Mark 15:34)

What kind of path was it that led him to this point, to the horror of this moment? That was Jesus. That was God's path to us, to the dark place to which we all belong, because we have abandoned God and abandon him again and again. Sent by his father, Jesus went and came to us and thus to this place of God's wrath and seclusion. Why is that? Simply and clearly, in order to take the place of each one of us, to be the object of God's wrath and be abandoned by God—so that, except for him, no one has to be in that position! He entered the godforsaken state that was our due, in order to take it upon himself, to bear it, and to take it away with the divine power given to him. He cried out, "My God, my God, why have you forsaken me?" in order that we might no longer have to ask that question. Certainly, no life lacks moments, hours, days, weeks, perhaps years, in which we don't believe we can ward off the idea that we would like to be abandoned by God—we who have so often abandoned God. One and all, we are mistaken, however, if we feel and think that way. In the light of Good Friday, the state of being godforsaken can only be a shadow, only a pale memory, only a bad dream. It could well be true, but it is not true—not for you and not for me or for anyone—that God has forsaken us.

Easter

When it was evening . . . Jesus came and stood among them.
(John 20:19)

And what a coming it was! Out of the realm of death's dominion, which overpowers all human beings—out of the grave! This is how the one who came that day and stood in the middle of his disciples climbed onto the throne befitting him in the middle of all of world history. At that time Jesus wished, brought, and created peace and a good day for all people of all nations and times, for the whole visible and invisible world. Into the middle of the whole of humankind—now shouting to high heaven, now gloomy unto death—the crucified and resurrected Jesus came that day with power and might as the Lord of all. Into the middle of all the illnesses and natural catastrophes; all the wars and revolutions; the peace treaties and the violations of peace; into all the progress; stagnation, and regress, into all the deserved and undeserved human misery, it happened in his time that he revealed himself as who he was, is, and will be: "Peace be with you" (John 20:21). What happened on that day became, was, and remained the center around which everything else moves. For everything lasts its time, but the love of God—which was at work and was expressed in the resurrection of Jesus Christ from the dead—lasts forever. Because this event took place, there is no reason to despair, and even when we read the newspaper with all its confusing and frightening news, there is every reason to hope.

God's Presence

Jesus came and said to them, ". . . I am with you always."
(Matt. 28:18, 20)

Jesus Christ is not without his own. He is who he is by being in the middle of them: the saving and illuminating center, and they form the circle saved and illuminated by him. This, then, cannot mean that the activation of our freedom is played out in a sphere where our relationship to Jesus Christ is reduced to a mere looking back on his presence in the past and looking forward to it in the future. In particular, it is not a question of Jesus Christ being dependent even temporarily on having himself represented by a worthy Christendom. Human beings, then, are not left to themselves but confronted by the Reconciler, who in his superior freedom even now, even here comes again, and in this very confrontation and in all their problems they are upheld, covered, comforted, nourished, and led. Because he meets us in the middle of our everyday lives and is with us every day, he is the hope of all of us. It is certain that even the day we are living today is a day of the living Jesus Christ. It may be that it is also a day in which we sin, a day in which the earth is covered with so much suffering, a day of the devil and demons. What is crucial, however, is that it is also a day of Jesus Christ. Nearer than any other person, he is the neighbor of every person, the compassionate Samaritan of us all. His day is really ours; our day is his.

God's Promise

My grace shall not depart from you.
(Isa. 54:10, Luther)

This means: I the Lord am good to you—not only good from far away—but, rather, I the Lord turn to you and do so not as a mere gesture and with empty hands. I the Lord will look after you, and—what's more—I the Lord will now take your concerns, the concerns of your life into my hands, make them my own concerns, and thus make them good. Because you are such a fine person? Because you have earned it? No, no. Not for that reason! But because I so choose and want to be gracious to you. "My grace" means this: you are a downright useless servant, but as such I want to take you into my service. You are a highly doubtful friend to me—my enemy more often than my friend!—but I want to be your good friend, your best friend. You are a disobedient child (oh yes, we are all only God's disobedient children), but I want to be a faithful father to you. That is the grace that will not depart from you. Why not? Simply because it is grace and thus absolutely not dependent on you—because it is my grace, not human but divine grace! Therefore it cannot and will not depart from you. For you it may be a hidden grace, but it will not depart from you. For you it may and must be largely a hard and strict grace that also will sometimes hurt you, but it will not depart from you.

When it comes to grace, we are all ungrateful bunglers, but grace will not depart from you or from me or from any of us!

God's Claim

For your law is my delight.
(Ps. 119:77)

The commandment of God is distinguished from all other commandments in that it is permission: it is the granting of a certain freedom. All other commandments mean that from somewhere we are told what to do—if not to say, hassled and plagued from one side or another—and the worst of all is when we begin to impose commandments upon ourselves. On the whole, these commandments express a mistrust of human beings: it might be dangerous to give them freedom; they will certainly misuse their freedom. So these commandments impose anxieties from various sides. They accost people with these anxieties; they put fear into people and hold them in fear. Their bidding is essentially a forbidding; it is the refusal of all possible permissions.

The commandment of God, however, sets human beings free. The commandment of God gives permission. This is the only way it commands. Even when God's commandment and the other commandments say the same thing, it is not the same thing at all. The commandment of God will not compel people; rather, it will burst the bonds of compulsion under which they have lived. It will not meet them with mistrust but with trust. It will appeal not to their fear but to their courage, and it will instill in them not fear but courage. This is true because the commandment is the shape of God's grace: the gentle yoke and the light burden, and to take them on simply means our enlivenment. God prepares this for us by giving us his commandment.

The Wanted Creature

Plants and Trees

"Let the earth put forth vegetation . . . and fruit trees."
(Gen. 1:11)

The world of plants putting forth shoots in obedience to God's word will not remain the only living creation, but it is the first one and the presupposition for all others. All creatures are alive, which is something they have in common with plants, and they stay alive by finding their nourishment in the world of plants. This covered table stands necessarily in the middle of the house built by God. Human beings do not need to look around with concern. God provided for them before he created them. They should also observe that they will not be in a position to take what they need on their own. "These all look to you to give them their food in due season" (Ps. 104:27). The creation, by taking place in this order, made any prideful, high-handed interference by human beings impossible. Without them and before they existed, there were plants and trees. They also have their own worth and right to life. Only then, after them, were human beings put in place, through God's will and word, as beneficiaries of the plants' and trees' surplus. So, when they started to live, human beings lived and live through God's grace, precisely by living from this table already spread, before they came along. And thus every bite with which people nourish themselves is a sign of grace, but not just a sign; it is itself the grace in, with, and under which human beings are allowed to live and without which they would not live. Will their sovereignty over plants and animals consist in anything other than the fact that they have more to be thankful for than these other creatures of the earth?

Fish and Birds

"Let the waters bring forth swarms of living creatures, and let birds fly above the earth."

(Gen. 1:20)

Here we are concerned with the sea and the air and thus with places that are by nature far from and foreign to human beings, places where they can stay either not at all or only artificially and temporarily, places that are dangerous because they are close to the element of chaos. Even there the lives of independent creatures begin through the creative command of God. So deep below and so far above, God wants to begin his work on and with such beings. So mighty is his mercy. So much is he Lord and Master of the whole universe and thus even of those border regions. God says, let there be swimming and flying things where human beings already think they see the jaws of death opening up. Even there they are offered a spectacle that inspires confidence. Fear for life in face of the monstrous nature of the created realm must obviously give way; living courage for the venture of existence in this realm must obviously awaken when this spectacle finds open eyes and the witness of the fish and the birds is perceived. If such endangered populations are already living, then the much more secure human population can also confidently do the same. If there are no monsters there, if human beings, when looking there, find themselves simply among distant friends and relatives, what do they have to fear on the solid ground where God created them? What can frighten them here, if there is nothing to frighten them there?

Animal Friends

God made the wild animals of the earth.
(Gen. 1:25)

The biblical creation saga sees human beings in association with the company of tame, creeping, and wild animals. If it is true that people are more noble than these, it is also true that they need these creatures, while animals do not need people at all. They and they alone will be deemed worthy of being God's partners in the covenant of grace. In all of this, however, they will have these companions, the animals, beside them. Everything that happens between God and human beings involving events and life and death will also be accompanied in the animal kingdom; in this happening it will have its witnesses, who will not also remain dumb when human witnesses fail, and who will sometimes speak louder and more urgently than all human witnesses. Human well-being and disaster, human joy and suffering, will be reflected in the weal and woe of this, their animal environment. The animals—not as independent partners of the covenant but as companions of human beings in the covenant—will be comrades of their promise and also of the curse that shadows their promise. Full of fear but also full of certainty, the animals will wait with human beings on their fulfillment and with them will breathe a sigh of relief when it has happened in a preliminary way and when it happens in a final way.

Reverence for Life

God . . . breathed into his nostrils the breath of life.
(Gen. 2:7)

All human life is, as such, surrounded by a special solemnity. As such, it wants to be deemed valuable in ever new amazement. It is a question of everyone treating their own existence and that of every other person with reverence. Human life does not itself create such respect. Rather, when human beings, through faith in God's word, become aware that and how God, from eternity, has chosen and loved them in their little existence, and what he has done for them in time, then in human life they are faced with the call to reverence, because the living God himself has looked after them in this spirit. One thing is certainly true: the birth of Jesus Christ is the revelation of the commandment of reverence for life. It gives to human life, even in its most dubious form, the character of being unique, one of a kind, unrepeatable, and irreplaceable. Reverence for life decides that it is a good thing to be allowed to be a human being. It characterizes life as the incomparable and unrepeatable opportunity to praise God. In this way life is exalted as an object of reverence. As the reverence asked of human beings, it is not immeasurable. Life is not a second God, and thus the reverence owed to it is not equal to reverence for God. Rather, it is limited by what God wants to have from the human beings he has chosen. Indeed, their life belongs to him. He lends it to them.

Male and Female

Male and female he created them.
(Gen. 1:27)

God exists in community. Because he is not lonely within himself and thus does not want to remain outwardly lonely, it is, therefore, not good that human beings should be alone. In its basic form, humanity is co-humanity. That this is so is obvious, since we cannot say human being without having to say either man or woman and without at the same time having to say man and woman. For the man the woman is, for the woman the man is, in the extreme sense, the other person, the fellow human being. To see and be seen by this other person, to talk to and listen to this other person, to experience support from and to give support to this other person, must mean the greatest human need, but also the greatest human problem and the greatest human fulfillment. The one should and must know him- or herself asked by the other: can and will you vouch for the fact that your kind is also human? Can you show this to me in such a way that I can also understand it? There must be a great deal that is typically male that simply remains unsaid and undone, or that is said and done quite differently when a man realizes that he is supposed to prove himself as a human being in the eyes of a woman, for whom he is such a big question mark. And the very same thing would also have to be said about feminine talk and actions. For both there is only an accidental, external, temporary, and passing state of being alone and for oneself. Their being is in truth always and under all circumstances a being with another person.

Life Together

Do not deprive one another.
(1 Cor. 7:5)

Human beings enter into marriage and live in the state of matrimony because they have recognized that God especially expects this of them and that for this reason they can and must do it. The call to marriage is the call to such a life together. Marriage is more than love. Marriage is the testing of love. For in marriage, namely, it is a question of repeating the yes of love in real life. "In real life" means living in the realities of daily life: work and worry, joy and suffering, health and sickness, youth and old age, while dealing with the small and large, internal and external, individual and social questions—but then somehow everything with each other, everything in special devotion to each other, everything in step with each other. Life together, however, does not mean something like lockstep. For they have "freed" themselves for the special thing that they each are. Marriage is community in this mutually granted freedom that is lived on each side. It is a question of freedom in community. Marriage as life together means remaining within the orientation of one particular man toward one particular woman and vice versa. Faithful love means that one is concerned with this other person—with one's total self and with the other person in his or her total self. Then an atmosphere will also be created, a "home" will be built, which can become an inn, a refuge, perhaps for many others, and its secret consists entirely in that deepest joyousness that at its most intimate—strictly between two people—is an event and becomes an event again and again.

Children

Children are a gift of the Lord.
(Ps. 127:3, Luther)

Parents live for their children, so that they may be guardians of their children, in the confidence that God is the one who vouches for them, as he does for the parents. God is their spokesman; God is their caregiver; God is the one who in truth lives for them. The parents themselves, with all that they can be and do for their children, are only God's witnesses. True parental authority is exercised so that the children become aware that the parents themselves live under an authority. Even authority can ultimately be only witnessed. The parents must consider the fact that their task is a limited one. They cannot even make their children healthy in body and soul, much less make them "happy," much less make them "competent people," much less make them creatures pleasing to God or make them Christians. They can make nothing of them at all. They can only do their best, which, however, will never reach into the heart of the lives of their children—in order then to have to stand humbly by in view of what God wants of the children and in view of their own highest development in this or that direction. While doing all they can and must do in their responsibility, parents can only place their children in God's hands, from which they have received them. And that will ultimately be the best that parents can do for their children: when they consider—and act accordingly—that the Holy Spirit is the real doer of the good, to which they as human beings can only lead their children.

Youth

Rejoice, young man, while you are young.
(Eccl. 11:9)

One could call youthful, in the good sense of the word, a deed in which obedience to God's commandment made itself known in a special way as a step from the past into freedom. Even the young person already has, perhaps, strong impressions but still little experience. There are older people who have only too much. The fact that young people are still relatively inexperienced can mean the possibility that no one has suggested to them that they should already be creatures of habit, experts, traditionalists or blasé individuals, relativists, or skeptics. They should actually still be capable of a certain independence and also a certain fruitful amazement. They should still have little reason to be seriously disillusioned or downright vexed vis-à-vis all too many people. Also they really should not still have to be bored. And the idea of a fate that blindly governs their life should actually still be foreign to them. Because they may still be less impressed by what is old, they may find what is new in the commandment even more enlightening in its newness. They may still have the energy for obedience. When they do that in a natural and open way, which should be characteristic of young people, then they act youthfully and should be an example for older folk, who in this very sense should also think young, in order to be obedient to God's command.

Adulthood

When I became an adult, I put an end to childish ways.
(1 Cor. 13:11)

The middle years of life offer a very special opportunity to be mature. It could be that the eye of the no longer young and not yet old person is especially free from the fog that, for the young person, can still veil the urgency of decision—and from the shadows that can do the same for an old person. Those in their middle years can come to a sudden realization: "It's now or never!" The sowing lies way in the past; now it's time for the harvest. The run-up has been done; now it's time to jump. The preparations have been made; now only the venture of the work itself actually remains. They have already lived, and they can still live. They now have a still considerable past and thus experience, but that should not yet have made them tired and stiff. Also they already see the end from some distance away and know that "night is coming when no one can work" (John 9:4). They see it, however, still at such a distance that the idea tempts them neither to resignation nor to a last-minute dash; rather, it should only urge them on with all deliberate speed. Thus they could also be especially free for the now and for the commandment of God that claims them in their now, both retrospectively and in anticipation of the future. Their position in the middle of life, between the times, has the character of both broadening and gathering. Will they recognize and seize their opportunity?

Old Age

So even to old age . . . do not forsake me.
(Ps. 71:18)

What would the wisdom of old age seriously mean? Speaking as Christians, we can say quite positively that it is especially older people who have the extraordinary chance to have to live—no, to be allowed to live—on the basis of what earlier they often enough sang happily from Luther's famous hymn: "Did we in our own strength confide, Our striving would be losing; Were not the right Man on our side, The Man of God's own choosing." Now it could practically become enlightening to them that, actually, up until now they have already, in fact, lived solely from God's free, unearned mercy, and that all of their own free decisions and deeds were precisely worth only as much as they were able to gain from this strange light that fell on them from outside. For them the right time may now have come for the "existential" understanding of the doctrine of justification. For this very reason, however, it may then have also brought a new and final time for their own free decisions and deeds—precisely in the happy hope of that strange light! And thus it may also be the right time finally to see that this strange light also shines over the known course of the world and over all the "peoples" so thoroughly illuminated by it, and thus the right time to become openminded again in all directions, as well as a little more lenient, and then also, for this very reason, more helpful.

A Crazy World

Empty Hands

"He has filled the hungry with good things."
(Luke 1:53)

Our Father in heaven, our life is so confused. Show us the order that you gave it and want to give it anew. Our thoughts are so scattered. Gather them around your truth.

Our way lies so dark before us. Go ahead of us with the light you promised us. Our conscience accuses us. Let us know that we may rise in order to serve you and our neighbor. Our hearts are restless within us. Lord, give us your peace. You are the source of everything good; you yourself are the good, and beside it there is no other. You do not want people to seek you for themselves and endeavor solely to solve their own problems. You want us, in our misery and in our hope, to be one united people of brothers and sisters. As such a people we ask you now to give us your hand, so that together we may thank you and that together we may again and again stretch out our so empty hands to you. Amen.

Divinity Displaced

"All who exalt themselves will be humbled."
(Matt. 23:12)

This is the divine humility and, precisely in its demonstration, the incomprehensibly great and marvelous deed of God: God becomes and is like us. But we—for whom God in this way is God—we want to be like God. Human sin is human arrogance; it involves human deeds that do not correspond to the divine deed in Jesus Christ, but contradict it. It is indeed not true that God is the kind of Lord with whom to want to trade places would make any kind of sense. It is indeed not true that it could oppress human beings even in the slightest way to be servants of God. For God is from the beginning their really and totally gracious Lord, who not only does not withhold salvation from them, but gives it in abundance. What is more, God wants to have them participate as his servants in his governing. How we humans deceive ourselves in the process of such an absurd confusion—above all about God! By making our own choice to pass by the grace of God and shake off our responsibility toward him, we choose what in itself is nothingness. We make God into the devil. For if a devil "exists," he is identical with the boundary concept of a lone, autocratic, and thus "absolute" being. And it cannot be denied that human beings, by choosing this orientation, sell themselves to the devil and "go to the devil." This is what the human beings look like with whom God has reconciled himself in Jesus Christ. He has answered their undertaking with the corresponding countermeasure: he humbled himself.

Humanity Enslaved

"You will be like God."
(Gen. 3:5)

It is absurd that human beings want to be God. When they want that, they become inhuman. It is precisely as God's servants that they are allowed and able to be essentially and completely human. How they quarrel with themselves when they rebel against this arrangement! When they think they can exalt themselves, they fall into the abyss. In their act of rebellion, the servants become slaves. Their actions disrupt and distort the relationship between Creator and creature, between God and humanity. In a real way it is transformed into an undignified farce and thus, in the realm of created being, produces the greatest confusion conceivable. It creates an illusory world in which "down" becomes "up," the great "before" becomes a small "after," every norm becomes false, every word a contradiction, and every deed wrong. Immediately the world of creatures is also affected. There can be only one result: the people over whom God wants to be Lord will reach for dominion over other people, and they will be met with the same strivings. The battle over power—the power of the two sexes, the power of individuals, of nations, of classes—must now begin, and with the battle comes the carrying out of a reciprocal judgment, which will be a judgment without grace. That means, however, the invasion of chaos into the realm of creation.

51

Masterless Powers

"Everyone who commits sin is a slave to sin."
(John 8:34)

The alienation of human beings from God directly involves their being alienated from themselves, which means that they begin to exist without a master. Not that their masterless state can in any way alter the fact that God is their God! For human beings, however, it is bad enough that they would like to undertake such a flight into being masterless. The various forms of their own ability now turn against them, as they themselves have against God. Their capabilities now become powers wreaking havoc without a master. World history is also the history of countless absolutisms powerful enough to get beyond the control of those who might and should be their master. No invoking of human freedom helps here: such absolutisms are the true engines of society. One of these masterless powers is mammon. In its whole innate lack of worth, money seems to be the epitome of all human values—not money as such but the money that human beings intend to have, while in truth it has them, and it has them because they want to live without God. We do not notice the number of dependencies of this kind in which we all exist. It would be better, however, if we noticed what kind of game is being played with us, because we would then know what we are doing when we pray "Thy kingdom come"—namely, that we are asking for the gracious exposure and ultimate removal of these absolutisms that control us.

Loneliness

"Where is your brother Abel?"
(Gen. 4:9)

How can human beings seek and find their brother or sister among fellow human beings if they want to keep God from being their father? The necessary consequence of their lack of communication in the vertical dimension is their lack of communication and their loneliness in the horizontal dimension. Without the knowledge of God there is no meaningful togetherness of human beings, no genuine collaboration, no genuine sympathy, no genuine shared joy, no genuine society. And work that is not collaboration is bustling idleness. Joy that is not shared joy is empty delight. Suffering that is not sympathy is dull pain. The human being who is not a fellow human being is inhuman. If we are without fellow human beings, then we are against them. We must, however, also see the reversal: if in my loneliness I choose the other person over myself, then I enter the realm of a still more fearful loneliness in which God can no longer be God for me. If I succeed in despising people, then even my so willingly and joyfully produced praise of God will stick in my throat. If I am merely an exploiter of my neighbor, then I will certainly believe that I can also simply use God, and I will make the painful discovery that God does not find pleasure in that. I have already hated God and reviled and offended him; I have already waged war against God, if I have done all that against my brother. If I am inhuman, then I am thereby also godless. God without our fellow human being is just an illusion, an idol.

53

Spinning Our Wheels

"Let us build ourselves . . . a tower with its top in the heavens."

(Gen. 11:4)

Are all the means of speeding up traffic that we are offered today really indispensable? We think they are indispensable because of the time that they save us. It's as if the rational people of bygone days with slower traffic did not have enough time for what was really necessary—and as if the irrational people of our day, with all the speed of our traffic, still did not have enough time for what is necessary. We can and we want to accomplish a great deal—and more and more—but by and large we are really just spinning our wheels, because we want to have and use a power that we basically don't need at all, and perhaps for our salvation we would in some ways be better off if we had never learned about it, much less unleashed it. It was bound to happen: the power that exceeds our real necessities of life, the power of technology—which basically has its own rationale and purpose, and which, in order to survive and be able to improve itself, must call forth ever new problems to solve—this power had to become the monster that it largely is today, and ultimately, absurd though it is, it had to become a technology of disruption and destruction. Yet people should not accuse technology of "having no soul"; it is rather people themselves and their irrational will to power that have no soul. The real problem with modern technology is people themselves.

The Struggle for Existence

Out of the slavery their cry for help rose up to God.
(Exod. 2:23)

That work is to be done is in accordance with the commandment of God the Creator. When we do work, however, we take part almost inescapably in a contradiction against what is intended by this commandment. Here we must clearly understand that even in our best actions, we are twisted people in a twisted world. Human work may and must take place in collaboration. But precisely in the world of work, there is a struggle for existence, and there is inhumanity without and against our fellow human beings. One person wants to do it better here than another, because the one would like to have it better than the other, to the advantage of the one and the disadvantage of the other. Basically, to work properly is to work together. And the nourishing bread that is gained through work can only be bread that is shared with coworkers. If it were simply a question of everyone getting bread through work, then people would work side by side for their daily bread. The power of empty desires is the real social dynamite: the desire for an abundance that is not the beautiful abundance of life but only an abundance of nothingness. It is clear that the commandment of God will always be an exhortation to countermovements—to humanitarianism, to advocacy for the weak. And it is clear that this must come to expression in the voice of the Christian church. Its decisive word can only consist in the proclamation of God's revolution against all human "ungodliness and wickedness" (Rom. 1:18).

Stupidity

He has no pleasure in fools.
(Eccl. 5:4)

Sin is also stupidity, and stupidity is also sin. And stupidity here, strictly understood, means what is reprehensible, what the Bible calls "foolishness." The stupidity of human beings is expressed in the fact that although they believe they can find what is important in life without knowledge of God and without hearing and obeying his word, they never find what is important in life. They always come too early or too late. They always sleep when they should be awake, and they always get agitated when they should be asleep. They are always silent when they should speak, and they always talk when silence would be the better course. They always laugh when they should cry, and they always cry when they could confidently laugh. They always want to make an exception when the rule must be followed, and they always subject themselves to a law when they should choose freedom. They always work when only prayer will help, and they always pray when only work will help. They always quarrel when it is not necessary but harmful, and they always speak of love and peace when they could easily go at someone. They always speak of faith when they need to express a little sound human reasoning, and they always try to be rational when they can and should put themselves and others confidently into God's hands. Stupidity is very clever at believing everything at the wrong time, saying everything to the wrong people, and regularly neglecting the simple, the necessary, and what is required right now, in order with certain instinct to want and to do what is complicated, what is superfluous, and what at the present moment would only be disruptive.

Lies

They exchanged the truth about God for a lie.
(Rom. 1:25)

Human lies happen when human beings try to avoid Jesus Christ, the true witness who meets them. The serious avoider, who hides within us all, does not deny the truth. Indeed, the liar does not deny the truth—that is done only by beginners and those who have grown weak with age and returned to their beginnings. Those who lie with their full powers confess the truth, but it has become untruth, because in their mouths it is only the Christian truth as controlled by them. Now its offense is supposedly made harmless. It is made so by the lie. The real, juicy lie always smells of the truth. The real, juicy lie bears a face that radiates righteousness and holiness, wisdom and prudence, love of God and love of humankind. The lie is the specifically Christian form of sin. Once again Christendom has reason first to beat its own breast, in order then to be in a position also to call the common lie a lie, as well as to embrace profane truths with sincerity. It must have light within, if it is to become brighter in the world. In its very self, however, there will have to be destruction of the pious lie before there can be light. Initially the lie may go a long way among us. In the presence of Jesus Christ, however, it cannot even get started.

Speechlessness

When words are many, transgression is not lacking.
(Prov. 10:19)

Most of the words that we say and hear have nothing to do with a dialogue between I and thou, with the attempt to speak to each other and listen to each other. Most of our words, whether spoken or heard, are an inhuman, barbaric affair because we do not talk to each other and because we also do not want to listen to each other. We say them without wanting to seek each other, without wanting to help each other. And we hear them without wanting to find each other, without wanting to let ourselves help each other. This is the way we talk in private conversation and the way we speak in sermons, lectures, and discussions, as well as in books and newspaper articles. And this is what we hear and read. And thus are words reduced to mere words; we live in an inflation of words. Actually the words are not empty, but the people are, when they speak and hear empty words. Then the "I" also stands empty and idle when facing a "thou." But we must make it clear that the mistrust and disappointment here and everywhere are not the way to make things better. By being able to talk with one another and listen to one another, we at least have the possibility of encountering each other, and in any case, we stand already—or still—on the threshold of humanity. As long as we can talk and listen, there is nothing that keeps the spoken and heard word from being fulfilled by being put to proper use.

Illness

"Lord, he whom you love is ill."
(John 11:3)

Illness is an element of the rebellion of chaos against God's creation, an expression of the devil and demons. Over against God, it is powerless, because only as an element of what is negated by God is it real, powerful, and dangerous. Illness is a sign of the ruin from which there is no salvation other than through the mercy of God in Jesus Christ. Without or against God, there is nothing to be desired in this matter. Those who know that would have to respond to God's faithfulness with unfaithfulness, if in the face of illness they wanted to sit back and do nothing. They are supposed to want exactly what God has always wanted in the face of illness, as well as that whole dark kingdom: with God they must say no to it. To capitulate to it can never be obedience to God. A small drop of decisiveness in resistance to that kingdom and thus also to illness is better than a whole ocean of alleged Christian humility. What more is there to say? Only this: what we know as illness also has a deeply hidden form in which not only the power of the devil but also God's sincere good intentions are reflected. Then it is not a matter of capitulation to illness, but rather capitulation to God, who is also Lord over illness, who is also gracious to human beings even when he lets them fall ill. Then it is not a question of giving up the fight against illness, but of that fight including patience.

Let There Be Light!

O send out your light.
(Ps. 43:3)

O Lord our God and Father, we are thinking now of all the needs, great and small, of this present time and world of ours: of the millions of hungry people, compared to whom we have it so good; of the dark threat of the atomic bomb to our beautiful earth; of the perplexity with which the great statesmen and stateswomen face the task of speaking a reasonable word to each other; of the pain of the ill and the confusions of the mentally ill; of the many failures of our public order and of the insanity of most of our customs and habits; of all the vanity and going in circles that also exists in our intellectual and cultural life; of the insecurity and weakness also of our church life; of so much worry and complication in our family life; and also, finally, of all the particular things that may distress and burden each individual among us today.

Lord, let there be light! Lord, break, crush, and destroy all the power of darkness! Heal us, Lord, and we shall be whole—if it cannot yet be altogether, then in part and in anticipation, as a sign that you live and that in spite of everything, we are your people, whom you lead through everything to your glory. You alone are good. You alone are due honor. You alone can and will help us. Amen.

The Christian Life

The Open Door

In everything . . . let your requests be made known to God.
(Phil. 4:6)

That is the open door "to the beautiful paradise." It's not as if God needed to have us tell him what shadows torment us, but that we, like children, may take it to him in order to talk with him about everything that concerns us, large things and small things, important things and unimportant things, smart things and dumb things: "In everything . . . let your requests be made known to God." We can tell him how hard everything is for us, how puzzling things and people often seem to us, what we especially find wrong with ourselves, and how little we get along with others. We can make it known in prayer, which means with great and sincere humility; in pleading, which means with great childlike urgency and confidentiality; and in thanksgiving: we are thankful, first, that it is true and that we may know that through our Lord everything has basically already been put into order, and thankful, second, that we may come before him. And all of that together is our prayer that even in the midst of the shadow that still surrounds us, his face will not cease to shine on us, and that we will not grow weary of hoping that the fog and veil that still plague us may be ripped apart and moved aside.

The Little Sigh

"Lord, teach us to pray."
(Luke 11:1)

Is there a person who can rightly say: I can pray? I fear that the people who want to say that are in truth the very people who cannot pray. And, conversely, those who lament, "I cannot pray," are the ones to tell, "For this very reason, you are in truth very close to praying." Real praying is something that we cannot do, but something that happens—not on the basis of an ability, but because God has accepted us as his children. If we are his children, then we also cry out to him. The Bible's commandment orders us: Ask! Keep before your eyes our Lord Jesus Christ, who also prayed for us on the cross! You have nothing left to do but to accept his grace. When you say yes to the grace of God, then you are obeying the command; you are praying. This is the little sigh with which we say to God: Ah, yes! That is prayer and the source of all prayers. It includes the whole Lord's Prayer and every miserere and Gloria that the church has ever prayed. In this little sigh lies everything, and everything must ever and again become this little sigh. There is no art of praying. There is only the quite simple permission of the child of God. Making use of this permission is what you should do when you cannot pray.

Faith

"I believe; help my unbelief!"
(Mark 9:24)

The event of faith is a question of the word of God freeing one person among many to affirm this very word, not just as simply comforting and helpful, but also as obligatory for the world, for the church, and for that individual. It is comparable to the natural turning of a bud into a flower and its natural turning toward the sun or the natural laugh of a child who has just experienced something funny. It does not matter that as a rule it will be a rather weak faith that flickers with the gusts of life. Those who believe know that their faith cannot be based on their own strength and reason. They can do it only in spite of the unbelief that also resides within them. Thus they will not suppose that they *have* faith but only that they seriously put it into practice anew every morning, as the Israelites did with the manna in the wilderness. The question whether faith lies within someone's province is a reckless question. The serious question, rather, is whether people—when shown the work of God taking place and the word of God spoken also in their province, as well as the living power of the Spirit also operating in their province —can afford to persist with a barren attitude of "I lack faith." Or whether they will stop flirting with their own unbelief and live in the freedom given also to them.

Beginners

The steadfast love of the LORD . . . [is] new every morning.
(Lam. 3:22–23)

The Christian cannot very well become a believing, deadly serious representative of a point of view. Indeed, one can never *be* a Christian; one can only become one again and again: in the evening of each day rather ashamed of one's Christianity of that day and on the morning of each new day content that one may again dare to be a Christian—with comfort, with neighbor, with hope, with everything. The Christian church is agreed on one thing: that it consists purely of beginners—and that this is truly a good thing: to become small again, to begin from the beginning, and thus at no point to stand still. That is the unity of right belief. It is a question of faith, because all of that depends on Jesus, who alone is now able to make people into such simple, but happy beginners. It is a question of faith, because it requires a true miracle for people to let themselves be redeemed from the law, from compulsion, from solemnity, and from the evil seriousness of all points of view—even when they adopt one themselves. That is probably why there are so few Christians. This proves nothing against them. It would be terrible if there were only people who believed from a particular point of view. The few Christians have the beautiful task of showing the others that there is also another faith besides the "point-of-view faith."

Discipleship

Jesus . . . said to him, "Follow me."
(Matt. 9:9)

It is grace that confronts this man. And this confronting grace wants him to do something. Precisely because Jesus' command takes the form of the grace that concretely confronts us, it comes to us also in the sovereignty of the grace of which no one is worthy, which no one can choose, and therefore with respect to which no one can have reservations. The call to discipleship binds us to the one who is calling. Discipleship is thus not the adoption of a program or an ideal, nor is it the attempt to realize such a program or ideal. Jesus makes demands on us. He demands trust in him. Discipleship arises in faith and consists in the deed of rendering obedience to Jesus. The call to discipleship is always an appeal to take a certain first step in faith. For those called the call always means: Come out! Come out of the shelter of everything that is taken for granted and everything that seems useful and possible and promising for the future! And out of the shelter of a mere inner movement in which one in fact still does nothing, but only makes oneself important by taking things into consideration. The call to discipleship makes a break. The kingdom of God is revealed in this call into the revolution of God already achieved in the existence of the human being Jesus. Those who are called by Jesus must make their doing and not doing correspond to the revelation of this revolution. They would lose their souls precisely in their failure to perceive the public responsibility that they assumed in becoming disciples of Jesus.

Not So Timid

They left everything and followed him.
(Luke 5:11)

Christians are people who have found their Lord, and consequently he has found them. They have no reason to need other lords. That does not mean that they are disrespectful people, but rather that they are liberated from all slavery, magic, and dictatorship: from their newspaper, from the judgment of people, from the currently prevailing mood and public opinion, from certain strong personalities, ideologies, principles, systems—and not least of all from the notion of the absolutely normative significance of their own convictions. In all weakness they have the power to fear and to love God above all things. Therefore, they are people who have only one concern: they could think too little of God, of his love and his power; in view of him and his command, they could expect too little and be too timid in thoughts, words, and deeds; they could dare too little. Otherwise they need to have no fear: not of the future, not of the overpowering stupidity and evil of anyone else or of their own, not of getting old, of being alone, or of dying, not of any fate or any devil. Certainly, they miss opportunities every day to make use of this power of theirs. And fear certainly tries constantly to overpower them. But they have power over it, and they can activate that power.

Standing and Walking

[The lame man] stood and began to walk.
(Acts 3:8)

Christians—the very creatures who are the first to know that as creatures they can only be dust under God's feet—are with God in faith, even if they have only a miserable little shred of real faith. And thus they are not under or in, but above the warp and woof of world events. They are the ones who are with God as children of the Father, as heirs of his glory; here and now they are already free masters of all things. They see even where there is nothing to see. They laugh about false visions and images of the world, even where these still have great power. They stand and walk, even when neighbors—and they themselves—think they see themselves falling into the abyss. They are brave, patient, and happy, even when not only the appearance but the whole massive reality of the world speaks against the possibility of being brave, patient, and happy. They are defiant, and not in some kind of artificial spasm from religious overexertion, but because by being able to believe, they themselves encounter defiance, and because it is held against them and against the whole world. Because they have their Master, they can, may, and must be defiant and be master with him. Out of the "therefore" immediately comes the "nevertheless," and what they still lack, what they still expect—longingly but without worry—is the revelation of their Lord as the Lord of world events, the revelation that their "nevertheless" is also a "therefore." That is what it means for Christians to live by their faith.

Christian Expertise

Great is our Lord . . . his understanding is beyond measure.
(Ps. 147:5)

Christians are the real experts in matters regarding God's world dominion. Naturally, they also confront anew every day the puzzles of the way the world operates, the profundities and the platitudes, the blinding lights and the dark areas of general creaturely events, to which their own life stories also belong. Naturally, they too have no master key to the mysteries of the great process of existence, which take on new forms every hour. On the contrary, they will be the very ones who know that all the master keys that people are supposed to have in hand are worthless. Of all people, they are the very ones who will repeatedly meet events as the most astonished, the most affected, the most startled, and even the most pleased. They are the very ones who, not as crafty characters who always anticipate everything and again are proven right, but rather as children in the forest or on Christmas eve, as those who are surprised again and again by encounters and experiences that happen to them, by the cares and duties laid upon them—they are the very ones who repeatedly find it necessary to begin again. All of that, however, is precisely because they know what it is all about. All of that is because they are in agreement with the place from which everything comes and from which directly or indirectly everything also comes to them: creatures with their Creator, children with their Father. That is Christian expertise in matters of divine world dominion.

Another's Burdens

Bear one another's burdens.
(Gal. 6:2)

No one can get rid of another person's burdens, or the nuisance that they cause. And they are precisely what we are not supposed to want to eliminate! Bearing one another's burdens means mutually suffering, enduring, and letting the reciprocal nuisance of burdens pass over us. Bearing means taking advantage of the permission and possibility of mutually forgiving the experienced nuisance. Bearing means treating each other in a kindly fashion, not as we do with rude and evil people, but as with those who are poor and sick—for example, as patients naturally do when they share the same room in a hospital. Bearing is thus the opposite of blindness and indifference with regard to mutual relapses and sins, but also the opposite of all indignant accusations and attacks at their sight. Bearing consists in the support that we mutually afford, so that we assume and take up each other's burdens as companions on the way that we have in common and can only travel to the end if we go together. Bearing also means discovering the beam in one's own eye and finding it a lot more interesting than the speck in a brother or sister's eye. In this way we give each other breathing space, whereas any other course can lead to new troubles. In this way things change—not everything but some things. By mutually carrying each other's burdens, we do in a small and individual way what Jesus did and does in a big way, as the Son of God and perfect Savior.

Love

[Love] does not insist on its own way.
(1 Cor. 13:5)

Christian love corresponds, after a fashion, to the deed of God's love. If that love is an emulation of divine love, then it is also deed. Loving means doing what is more blessed than receiving, namely, giving. Eros takes; those who love give. Not that they receive nothing! They are the most gloriously blessed on earth. But they enjoy that only through giving. . . . They give themselves. That sounds enormous, but in truth it is nothing special. In this way they only give away what can be theirs only when they give it away. They come out into the open like cave people, blinking a little because the sun is so bright, a little apprehensive because it's also windy and rainy, but they come out. Their lives will be eccentric, because their center is outside themselves. It is a question of dedication. This will include many kinds of giving, including the free giving of money and the dedication of time.

Where there is love, there is a little house of God in the middle of sinners. Those who genuinely love are certainly happy people. And genuinely happy people are also loving people. The blessedness of those who love is that they, as people loved by God who emulate his doing, may exist in fellowship with him, even when from the side of the loved ones, as from a stone wall, only an empty answer comes back or none at all. They love not for the sake of an answer, but because they are freed by God for this purpose.

Community

Let yourselves be built into a spiritual house.
(1 Pet. 2:5)

To build means to put together. Human beings need to be put together. For as human beings they are at first a pile that is pulling apart. For the achievement of individual purposes, people also like to be joined together, but for that very reason not entirely joined. They are gathered into the church for the purpose of all purposes, and thus their joining must be one that is absolutely sustainable—not a joining into a collective in whose existence the individual becomes of no importance, but a joining in freedom! Thus, putting together does not mean here the building of a seamless structure, but the building of a structure in whose joints the corners and edges of the individual building elements go together, so that they can mutually hold and support each other. Where two or three are gathered together in the name of Jesus, there they will know and recognize each other as those who are brought together by him. Love builds the church. Love consists in the fact that they— joined by God and by Jesus—also join themselves together, in order thus to be the community that can be used in service in the world. Just as a human being per se, without a fellow human being, would not be a human being at all, so also a Christian per se, separated from the communion of the saints, would not be a Christian at all. The royal freedom of one's faith is the freedom to be in community together with brothers and sisters in the property dedicated to that community and to be in the service commanded of that community.

Being Human

Permission to Live

"Because I live, you also will live."
(John 14:19)

You don't have to live at all, but you have permission to live. For living is a freedom granted by God. Wanting to live is indeed the will to live in this freedom in which human beings are not sovereign and are not lonely, but in every circumstance have God over them as the Creator, the Giver, and the Lord of their life. Why do you want to be sovereign and therefore lonely, and then certainly in this way or that discover sheer emptiness around you, then despair, and finally be driven to thoughts about suicide? All of that would be your lot only if you had to live, if life were not based on God-given freedom. But all of that has no point: God is gracious to you. What are the consequences of this? That you simply may live and—because God is God—can also live on the basis of the fact that he is gracious to you. That you therefore may simply accept that he is the sovereign and not you. He has and bears the responsibility for your life and not you yourself. He makes of it what he will, not what you imagine that you have to want. He justifies, sanctifies, saves, and glorifies you: that is not required of you. The only thing required of you is that you let the matter end there. Then you will find yourself surrounded by him on all sides; then you cannot despair: neither of yourself nor of your life, however unsuccessful and unfortunate or however useless it may seem to you. For you yourself are God's property, and therefore all of God's angels are with you.

A Good Time

My times are in your hand.
(Ps. 31:15)

Schiller was quite correct: "What you strike from the moment, no eternity will bring back." How do we know whether what we now knowingly or unknowingly strike out is only something small and dispensable and not the turn of events that could decide everything about our whole being in time, past and future? Now, this very moment, is not the time for dreaming, neither about what is past nor about what is coming. Now is the time to watch, the time to receive or to act, to speak or to remain silent, to say yes or no. Because by existing now, we are under God and in God's presence, there is therefore no avoiding the importance of the now and no excuse for missing or misusing the now. And, to be sure, there is, even in our now, no absence of God's grace and mercy. In all seriousness, that is what is joyous about our present time: because in it God is the one who is first and really present, we are not abandoned by him, not left to ourselves—not even in our feeblemindedness and stupidity, not even in our missing and misusing what is offered to us. Rather, in every moment we may rely on the fact that he forgives sins, protects straying children, and lets tired wanderers still take their stumbling little steps, that he is wise even about our foolishness, good even about our badness, awake even when we are really asleep and are dreaming of the past and the future, although we should be taking advantage of our present, which will never come again. Then, even though the special nature of his presence went unrecognized and unused or misused by us, he still will not have been present to us in vain.

Affirmed Limits

For everything there is a season.
(Eccl. 3:1)

When we say that through the sustenance of God creatures can continue to be, it means that they can exist within their limits as creatures. They can have their place in space, their moment in time. They can begin here and end there. They can come, stay, and go again. They can comprehend earth and not comprehend heaven. They can be free here and restricted there, open here and closed there. They can understand this but not understand that, do this but not do that, accomplish this but not accomplish that. The fact that they can have being in this way, within these limits, is neither imperfection nor dark fate. They have the freedom to have their own experiences and achieve their own goals, to do what they can and let that be enough. In this very freedom they are sustained by God. In this very freedom they come directly from God and go to God. In this very freedom they are ready to fulfill their destiny, namely, to live by God's grace through God's grace. Their opportunity comes precisely in the fact that they are here and now, that they are the way they are and not otherwise. And precisely by their letting this opportunity be right for them and by making proper use of it, they praise their Creator. "I will sing to the LORD as long as I live; I will sing praise to my God while I have being" (Ps. 104:33). Creatures do not run into imperfection or dark fate unless they praise God through their own power, unless they will not admit their limits or let them be right and proper.

Human Worth

You were bought with a price.
(1 Cor. 7:23)

Christians can, may, and should emulate the existence and activity of God for human beings—and the special distinction with which he treats them—in such a way that humanity itself becomes the special object of Christians' interest. This is precisely what they do when they simply look beyond everything else and toward human beings—who are loved by God in all their wrongness and wretchedness—when they let people be the real object of their interest and let their theme be the lives, the rights, the freedom, and the joy of all humankind. Their concern is people. They are born "humanists." Thus, their concern cannot be anything in and for itself but everything, with a view toward and a question about whether and to what extent it is beneficial or detrimental to the cause of human beings and their worth, which for the time being is relative. No idea, no principle, no traditional or newly established institution or organization can have an a priori claim on Christians' thinking, speaking, and intention. For when would a person become a wolf to other people in a more dreadful way than when one claims to approach them in the name of some kind of absolute? Because Christians are concerned about people, they can respond to all principles with only a relative yes or no. Therefore, they must resist all principles that claim incontrovertible validity.

Freedom

You were called to freedom.
(Gal. 5:13)

It is true that free people will also strive for independence, as far as that makes sense. But free people are not compelled to want independence by every external compulsion. They can also find all kinds of undesired discipline to be acceptable and pleasing.

We come closer to the heart of the matter when we describe freedom as human superiority vis-à-vis things that want to compel us from within. The words and deeds of free human beings reveal them to be people who always have under their control their respect for the importance of their own person, their fear of their inferiority, the tenacity of their high esteem for once chosen goals, and their concern for their good reputation.

The negation of slavery, even in its noblest forms, can never be more than a preparation for freedom. Free people are people who think and act positively; each is a sign of hope, of solace, of encouragement for many who are still enslaved. Thus they need freedom precisely for the benefit of those still enslaved.

Let us take a last step. It is not self-evident that there are free people. Freedom is a free gift. The origin of freedom is the free God, before whom all must confess themselves to be slaves, but who wants especially to look after slaves and has long ago accepted them. Again and again he creates new free people. And the truly decisive activity of their freedom consists in appealing anew every morning: "Lord, make us free!"

Fellow Human Beings

"It is not good that the man should be alone."
(Gen. 2:18)

Whoever sees people without fellow human beings does not see them at all. From the very beginning, from the first look and word, whoever does not know and take into account the fact that people have neighbors does not see them at all. We ask about the brightness of human beings in the light of the human being Jesus, in the light of the fact that the human being Jesus is for them. He is the Savior even of people who deny their humanity. This does not mean, however, that they have stopped being human beings, and that we are allowed or even bidden to interpret their very inhumanity as their humanity and to hold the work of their sin to be the work of God's good creation. The fact that they have their Savior in the human being Jesus is proof that they have not stopped being human. The fact that the Good Shepherd has also opened himself up for the benefit of his lost sheep shows that he still, as before, includes them in his flock. That is what makes the idea of a person without fellow human beings unbearable from the outset and not open to discussion. Any alleged humanity that is not, from the beginning, already co-humanity is inhumanity. The humanity of all people consists in the certainty of their being as being together with other human beings. When they exist not for themselves but in order to be together with other human beings, then they are concretely human, they fulfill their purpose of being God's covenant partner, they are the beings for whom Jesus exists, and therefore they are real human beings.

Foreigners

The LORD . . . loves the strangers.
(Deut. 10:17–18)

When God's commandment is heard loud and clear, the concepts of home, fatherland, and nation will prove capable of expansion. Those who live in obedience can, without becoming disloyal, also be at home in a foreign land. They will find their fatherland again, not where things go well for them, but anywhere that they are called to do good. And if they should encounter foreigners in the middle of their own people and land, then they will only be moved by this to reinforce the inner strengths of their own people and land in such a way that they not only can tolerate but also can benefit from much that is foreign—perhaps also from many foreigners who seek a second home in their land—and make it their own and part of their own lives both internally and externally. On the other hand, if foreign influences cannot be resisted in a land by means of inner strength as something actually better, it may not be worth the effort to defend against those influences by external means. In every land there are many native customs that could be greatly influenced or replaced by foreign people and their ways of doing things, and it would be a great gain. One's own people in their own space cannot and must not be a wall but only a door. It must never be bolted, much less walled up.

Insight

"What do you want . . . ?". . . "Let me see again."
(Mark 10:51)

The human sense of sight means that one person becomes visible to another eye to eye. The expression "that does not concern me" or "that does not concern you" is, under almost all circumstances, an unfortunate expression because, under almost all circumstances, it means that the being of this or that fellow human being is of no concern to me, and my being is of no concern to this or that person. I want neither to see that person nor to have that person see me; my openness has its limits in regard to that person. When we go outside of ourselves, when we do not refuse to know another person and are not afraid to be known by another person, to that extent we exist in a human way, even if otherwise we exist in the deepest depths of humanity. (It is not necessarily so, but it is a fact of experience that when one lives more in the depths than on the heights of humanity, one is much more human than on those supposed heights!) The involvement in which we quite simply allow ourselves to see and be seen is the first indispensable step into humanity without which none of the following steps can be taken. It is a great, solemn, incomparable moment when between two people there is now perhaps an "insight," that is, when they see into each other's eyes and discover each other!

Talking to Each Other

A gentle tongue is a tree of life.
(Prov. 15:4)

You and I must talk. You and I must listen. And that means talk to each other and listen to each other. That is the human understanding of language. Comprehensively, language means reciprocal expression and reciprocal perception of expression, reciprocal speech and reciprocal perception of speech. All of these many elements must be present. Thus, for the human understanding of the human mouth and the human ear, everything depends on human beings talking to each other and listening to each other; it depends on expression and speech being reciprocal. It is well known how we look past one another, and we also talk and listen past one another. When that happens, it always means that in fact we are not involved in the encounter and thus are not acting in a human way. Two people can speak very openly, thoroughly, and enthusiastically with each other, but if their words serve only their own needs, if in talking together they only want to confirm and further themselves, then they will surely not make contact with each other. A dialogue cannot come out of two monologues. Dialogue—and thus real meeting— begins only when and where mutually spoken words become the means of seeking another person and helping that person; that means helping to correct the embarrassment that one person causes another. Then we will not speak past one another but with and to one another.

A Frank Word

Against the Stream

Render service . . . as to the Lord and not to men and women.

(Eph. 6:7)

Nothing has happened to change the fact that Christians—even in the middle of their supposedly and perhaps even very consciously Christian environment—will always be strange and threatened creatures. No matter how much they may know themselves to be in solidarity with the world and behave as such, the way of Christians can never be the way of the world—least of all the way of a presumably Christianized world. From the standpoint of what moves within them, they will have to go their own way in matters both small and large, and therefore in what they think, say, and espouse, they will remain foreigners—sometimes conspicuously, sometimes less noticeably, but always and fundamentally foreigners—who will often give occasion for others to take offense. They will appear to some as all too ascetic and to others as all too unconcerned affirmers of life—here as individualists, there as collectivists; here as believers in authority, there as free spirits; here as bourgeois and there as anarchists. They will seldom be found in the majority prevailing in their surroundings. In any case, they will not be going with the flow. For them the great truths of conventional wisdom will never have absolute validity. Nor, certainly, will their absolute negation, and thus they will also hardly be able to count on the applause of current revolutionaries. And they will cultivate their freedom not only in free thoughts in private, but also in free and open deeds and modes of behavior that will never find public approval.

The Upper Hand

"The gates of Hades will not prevail against it."
(Matt. 16:18)

In all the whole world, there is only one possibility for the church: simply to be the church! The church means those who are around Jesus and whom he sees all around him. The church is Jesus' "circle": the group around him that in a totalitarian world is nourished solely by the word of God. And the more totalitarian the behavior of the world, the freer they are to believe and obey, because Jesus is there and the church stands around him. When it does this, then its existence is possible. Then the church is a bulwark of liberty, even when it is oppressed. Then the church has power and is perhaps the only power that exists in this world ruled by powers. The church has the wonderful opportunity to have the upper hand over the totalitarian world, not with a balled fist, but peacefully and happily. The church can also wait, and it knows that it does not wait in vain. The church knows that all of the totalities of the world—which are really false divinities—are lies. Ultimately one cannot be afraid of lies. The truth will out, and in the church, that can be known. The more the church lives in humility and knows that there is also much falsehood in ourselves, the more certainly it can also know that God rules—over the lies in us and over the lies in the world. Then the church can, in all circumstances, do its duty and forbid itself to be anxious about the future. Its future is its Lord.

Mission

"You are the light of the world."
(Matt. 5:14)

The church of Jesus Christ is there for the world. For this very reason it is there for God. Above all, God is there for the world. And since the church of Jesus Christ is primarily there for God, it can, for its part, do no other than to be there in its own way for the world. It saves and receives its own life by being involved in and giving itself for other human creations. The church, to be sure, is the people who are set apart from the world by the word of God. But it is really called out of the world only when it is called into the world. Coming from the table of the Lord and following his precedent, the church cannot refuse to sit at table with the other sinners, with all sinners. If it wanted to flee from the world, it would have to flee from the love of God. It would make itself equal to the world if its main concern was to protect its purity and not compromise it with the world. That's just it: the world believes that it can maintain itself by everyone wanting to satisfy their own needs. What it needs is not to be reinforced in its way once again by another variation of that way, but in unambiguous practice to be shown the way beyond that way. It is waiting for a Samaritan to appear in its midst. The Christian church itself is not the Samaritan who has come into the world as Savior. But it has been sent into the world to act in his service. In welfare and social work, the church makes its witness to the Savior clear as Samaritan service to be performed by the community for those who have fallen into the hands of robbers: with him who was neighbor to the lost. In service the church goes and does likewise (Luke 10:37).

Political Worship

Seek the welfare of the city . . . and pray to the LORD on its behalf.

(Jer. 29:7)

The church must remain the church. The Christian community has a duty that is not taken away from it by the civil community and which it cannot pursue in the forms used by the civil community. It proclaims the lordship of Jesus Christ and the hope of the coming kingdom of God. The civil community has no such message to impart, and it is not dependent on such a message being communicated to it. It does not pray, and it is not dependent on someone praying for it. In the very fulfillment of its own duty, however, the Christian community also participates in the duty of the civil community. By believing in Jesus Christ and proclaiming Jesus Christ, it believes in and proclaims the one who as the Lord of the church is also the Lord of the world. The Christian community prays for the civil community. By praying for it, however, Christians make themselves responsible to God for it, and they would not do it seriously if they did not, in their very prayer for it, also actively work for it. They serve God, and precisely therefore and thereby, they serve human beings. The Christian community is based on the knowledge of God, who as such became human and thus the neighbor of human beings. It follows inevitably that in the political realm and under all circumstances the Christian community primarily looks after people and not after some kind of thing or cause. After God himself became a human being, human beings are the measure of all things.

Getting Involved

Shout out, do not hold back! Lift up your voice!
(Isa. 58:1)

Making one's confession of faith necessarily means grap-
pling with present-day issues that are of great moment to
the church and to the world. This is done not for the sake
of those questions or for the sake of answers to them, but
for the sake of making a necessary witness to Jesus Christ
in the present. Thus, it is certainly done in every age, as if
it had never happened before. Today as surely as yesterday,
here as surely as there, the confession of faith has to witness
to Jesus Christ. It does this, however, always in view of what
has taken place. It does not speak to the situation; rather, it
speaks to the issue in the situation—in the particular situation that it has itself chosen and characterized. It speaks not
out of the spirit of the age, but to it and with it. Taking
sides—that is, placing one's own concern at the service of
some other cause—is one thing. Getting involved—in one's
own concern, on one's own initiative, because the witness
to Jesus Christ requires one to say yes or no—is another.
When a church out of pure anxiety—lest it be brushed by
a dirty fender, lest it give the appearance of taking sides—
never ever trusts itself to get involved, it had better watch
to see whether it has necessarily compromised itself with
the devil, who knows no dearer partner than a church that,
concerned about its good reputation and clean image, is
always silent, always meditating and discussing, always neu-
tral. A church that is all too worried about the really not
very threatening transcendence of the kingdom of God has
become a quiet puppy. That is what must not happen.

A Frank Word

Proclaim the message; be persistent.
(2 Tim. 4:2)

The Christian church knows to whom all power is given in heaven and on earth. For that very reason it knows how to distinguish between genuine and false earthly power, between authority instituted by God and authority arbitrarily invented by human beings and placed upon the throne. Therefore, the church is grateful for all genuine, proper power and for authority that is instituted by God, that sets limits on inhumanity, and that allows for humanitarian concerns. The Christian church must not be indifferent in this matter. It has all too often let itself be intimidated in this regard and remained silent when it should have spoken up. The Christian church cannot and should not want to become political itself. It can and must, however, bear witness to nations and governments that politics, worship, justice, and freedom are gifts of God. It can and must, in all frankness and love, ask, call, petition, and admonish when the state threatens to disintegrate or, conversely, to become paralytic, when it wants to serve injustice instead of justice, slavery instead of freedom, when it wants to move in too close on people or on God or on both. The Christian church is responsible for what happens and does not happen in the state. It owes the state a frank word. It is better for it to intercede three times too much for the weak than one time too little, better for it to raise its voice in an unpleasantly loud fashion than to speak with an agreeable, soft voice.

War and Peace

[They say,] "Peace, peace," when there is no peace.
(Jer. 6:14)

Making war does not belong among the normal duties of the state. Rather, its normal obligation is to maintain peace in such a way that life is served and war is kept far away. When a state does not properly pursue its normal duty, it will, sooner or later, find itself driven to the abnormal duty of war and then will also burden another state with this abnormal duty. When the object is not human beings but interest-bearing capital, whose maintenance and increase is the meaning and purpose of the political order, then the mechanism is already in operation that one day will send human beings off to kill and be killed. Then neither the alleged love of the masses for peace nor all the well-intended proclamations of idealists against war can help prevent the destruction of peace. With a peace that is not true peace, war may be inevitable. It takes little faith, reason, and courage to damn war in principle. And it takes no faith, reason, or courage to howl with the wolves that unfortunately war, like peace, belongs to the order of the world. It takes Christian faith, reason, and courage, however, to shout to nations and governments that peace is serious business: it is, namely, the business in which all time, all energy, all resources are to be invested, so that people may live and live with justice, so that there will be no reason to resort to war.

Rich and Poor

He has . . . sent the rich away empty.
(Luke 1:53)

When we hear that word "rich," we probably think of people who have a large pile of stock certificates and other
merry things of this kind. If other people hold the meaning of life to be in having and enjoying such things, then
they too belong to the rich. The rich, however, are all
those who make the claim that God and the people must
really be quite satisfied with them. But he sent them away
empty. He did nothing bad to them. He just left them
standing there with bag and baggage. He just had nothing
to say to them or give them. The poor rich!

Yet the poor rich can only act as if they were rich people. With their wealth they live in pretense to themselves,
to God, and to other people. In truth, none are satisfied by
what they themselves are and have. Thus, there is hope for
the rich. The poor rich should want to admit only one more
thing: God, be gracious to me, a sinner! Then with one
stroke, everything would be different. They would no
longer be the poor rich, but the rich poor. Then they would
hear what the angels said to the shepherds: "I am bringing
you good news of great joy . . . : to you is born this day . . .
a Savior" (Luke 2:10–11). He has turned the poorest people of all into the richest of all. He did that by becoming
their brother. Do you know what is the sure sign that people are rich poor people? They will be directly concerned
about the fact that there are millions in the world who lack
bread. They will then recognize these people as their
brothers and sisters, and they will act accordingly.

From Case to Case

Do not become slaves of human masters.
(1 Cor. 7:23)

In accordance with the confession, spiritually and theo-
logically obligatory positions of the church in the political realm are required when in a concrete disagreement
with a certain phenomenon the church is called upon by
the word of God in the practice of its service and in
responsibility to its faith. It does not have to deal time-
lessly with these or those isms and systems, but with the
historical realities that step into the light of God's word
and of faith. It is not obligated to some kind of natural law,
but to its living Lord. Therefore, it never thinks, speaks,
or acts "on principle." Rather, it judges spiritually and
therefore from case to case. Hence, it forgoes any sys-
tematization of political history and its own participation
therein. And thus it reserves for itself the freedom to eval-
uate new phenomena in new ways. If it did not travel a particular path yesterday, then it is not obligated to travel
farther on that path today. If it spoke yesterday on the
basis of its place and its responsibility, then it also can and
must remain silent today if, on the basis of its place and its
responsibility, silence is the better course of action. For
the unity and continuity of theological existence, it is best
if the church does not let itself be badgered into repeatedly being theological existence "today."

Public Welfare

I urge . . . prayers . . . for all who are in high positions.
(1 Tim. 2:1–2)

When I really pray, then I cannot remain inactive. Then I cannot simply say, "Oh, dear God, look out for . . ." Rather, when I pray—in this case for these persons in authority— I make myself responsible for them. Now it takes only a small step for me to be forced to recognize that I myself am also a person in authority. The people into whose hands the existence of the state is given are not only some authorities up above, but also those who are led or administered by these authorities. By political responsibility we understand that they have to pray for the existence of the state— indeed, they themselves are the state—and for what happens in the name of the state, but that they are also to work for it. All have to share in the responsibility for the existence of the state, for its reality, and for what is good or evil about it. It's a question of the maintenance of justice and peace. It provides a divine order for this purpose, and that is the justification for the state. The state has to serve the public welfare and thus justice, peace, and freedom—not the freedom of everybody to do what they want, but freedom understood precisely as the personal responsibility of all. The state has to promote and care for public welfare on the basis of freedom. Not a compulsory welfare, but a welfare that is sought and wanted and put into operation by all!

Under Way

God's Patience

The Lord . . . is patient with you.
(2 Pet. 3:9)

God is patient. Patience is when one person, waiting on another or others, lets them do as they like. The patience of God is his willingness—for the sake of his compassion and in assertion of his holiness—to leave others time and space for their own existence. God's compassion does not rule in such a way as to run over its object. Does this compassion not depend on the fact that there is a patience of God, this leaving room for sinful creatures with whom he gives himself room to talk and deal further? God has time. And his having time for us is what characterizes his whole activity in regard to us as an exercise in patience. God is not near-sighted; he knows very well what our physical makeup is. By knowing this, however, he has a real reason to be patient with us, the reason that he himself laid down. If he lets the many go their own ways, if he continues to give them time (and food for their time) and continues to wait for them in all of this, he does this for the reason that he has already come to them in the One. He does this because in the One, in whom he has given himself to all, they have already fallen into his hand. For the sake of this One, God is patient with the many. It's not as if they are given time and space in which to persist in their unrepentant state. Rather, God's patience grants them time to travel the road to faith.

Sabbath

Remember the sabbath day.
(Exod. 20:8)

The commandment of the sabbath day explains all the other commandments. For by requiring human beings to refrain from their own work, it explains that the commanding God, who has enabled and commissioned human beings for their own work, is the one who is gracious to them in Jesus Christ. It directs them away from all that they can accomplish themselves and back to what God wants to do for them. In its special nature, the sabbath day is a sign of what the meaning of all days is. The freedom, lack of worry, and absence of schedule that make up its special character would have to radiate also to the workday, on which these things could not happen as such—and so also the joy and openness to fellow human beings, without whom the Sabbath is actually inconceivable. When the workday is only a workday, a prison day, a day of worry, a day of schedules, only a day of bitter seriousness, only a day of self-help and self-justification, what kind of example does that set for a Sunday? And how can the workday be a proper workday? Those who believe on Sunday can also do it on a workday. They will work during the week materially and diligently, but neither as master nor as slave of their work. They will keep their eyes on one goal after the other and yet not become a slave of mammon. Even while quarreling every day, they will have peace and keep peace and pray, even as they work every day. They will both have themselves completely in hand and give completely out of their hand. Also, on workdays they will never be anxious. Why not? "We do not belong to ourselves, but to the Lord." And that needs to be practiced on the sabbath day.

Work

Take courage, all you people, [and] work.
(Hag. 2:4)

In all fields of human work it is generally a question of people wanting to eke out a living. What people crucially need for their existence can only be given to them by God. At least in healthy days, however, they themselves have the time and ability to see to the guarantee of their existence. Here people endeavor to earn their own living. Here it is a question of their own active affirmation of their existence. Here they take themselves in hand. Whenever people take themselves in hand, however, they run the risk of taking themselves captive and letting themselves be taken captive. Thus, their work must be protected from exposing them to this threat. If their work is to be done right, they need relaxation. Work done under tension is unhealthy, evil, contrary to God, and destructive of human beings. Then the cooperative nature of proper work tends to get lost. Then the image of a justified claim to life becomes blurry, and people fall victim to empty desires. Then they also tend to forget to ask about the difference between meaningful and meaningless purposes of work. Then they are no longer capable of working competently. Tension turns work into misery. We can let ourselves be liberated from the compulsion of such work. Human beings can and should work. They can and should actively affirm their existence, yet only with a view to the fact that it is already affirmed by their Creator, and in the relief that comes from this knowledge.

A New Start

*Those who wait for the LORD shall renew their strength . . .
they shall run and not be weary.*

(Isa. 40:31)

A fresh start takes place when something has become out-dated and must be left behind like the past night, and in its place something new is announced; it is like the coming of a new day. The model that has not been illuminated and considered enough is the exodus of Israel from Egypt into its promised land. A decisive farewell is said there to what is familiar and now still very near, which perhaps also had its advantages (say, in the form of the famous flesh-pots of Egypt). And decisive attention is given to something distant and affirmed in hope, which, nonetheless, has the disadvantage—even in its marvelous form—of being totally unknown.

In starting out anew, the church has made a choice. It has forbidden in advance any homesickness for what it is leaving behind. It welcomes and already loves what lies before it. It is still here, but no longer here; not there yet, but already there. It has a long journey before it, as well as battles, suffering, hunger, and thirst. There is no denying that it is sighing, but still more undeniably, it is rejoicing. And it thinks, speaks, and acts accordingly. The new start of the church consists in this crisis of the still captive, already liberated people of God.

Our Cross

Rejoice insofar as you are sharing Christ's sufferings.
(1 Pet. 4:13)

The cross that Christians bear when they follow Jesus comes without their wanting it or doing anything to get it. No one needs to worry that it will not come. We only need to be concerned that we not stubbornly or cleverly refuse to take it up, and that we not take it up halfway and then hastily drop it again. We only need to be concerned that though we will certainly have to suffer anyway, we might then suffer like the godless, without the comfort and promise of suffering with Jesus. Christians will have to pray that this does not happen, that the Holy Spirit will set them free to welcome the cross destined for them. The instruction to do so is not an ultimate but a penultimate word. The nature of the cross borne by Christians is such that it has an aim and thus also an end. It means setting limits, and therefore it is painful. But this limit-setting itself is not unlimited. Borne in our participation in the suffering of Jesus, it ends precisely where the suffering of Jesus points in the power of his resurrection and where our suffering also points with his. It is not our cross that is eternal, but the life that is opened by the death of Jesus on the cross. "When winter snows are gone, the beautiful summer comes again; so too after the pain, those who can expect it will rejoice" (Paul Gerhardt). In the meantime, also, there can be no lack of joy in the anticipation of this expectation.

Challenge

I am like a lonely bird on the housetop.
(Ps. 102:7)

Religion may be a private matter, but the work and word of God are the reconciliation of the world with God that occurred in Jesus Christ. God, however, has not spoken his last word in this matter. Namely, he has not spoken universally of the act of God that took place in Christ and in such a way that all ears, all minds, and all hearts would have to perceive it. That means that Christians stand over against most other people in relative loneliness. When things get serious, they will be able to see themselves as members of an almost disappearing minority. This isolation needs to be endured. What, then, should the little Christian band do? What does it want to do? What do these people expect at the great fair, on the great battlefield, in the prison and the madhouse, other than that the life of humanity will be presented again and again? What is the divine power of the gospel, praised by Paul, compared with the powers of the state, the world economy, natural science, and technology? It would be like sticking one's head in the sand if Christians did not find themselves challenged by all of that—and even deeper in the sand if, in order to avoid this question, they wanted to draw back into their own faith and loving. Yet in view of this limitation, undaunted hope is meaningful and advisable; that is, the day of the coming of Jesus Christ to full revelation will most certainly be the day when they— the living and the dead—will hear his voice.

Passing Away

The world and its desire are passing away.
(1 John 2:17)

Because he comes, and in him the mystery of glory, therefore it must be true that the world is passing away. Before him the world and its desires cannot prevail. When he comes, not only the evil world but also the good world will come into judgment. Because he comes, it cannot therefore be otherwise: now there are shavings; now there is debris; now he takes one thing after another from our hands. You think: I have to keep this or that, because it will move me forward. And then he who is coming says: no, that will not move you forward; that will hold you back. Give it to me! Get rid of it! You think: this or that is good for me and my health, and he who is coming says: no, that is not true; that will make you sick. Give it to me! Get rid of it! You think: this or that is true and clear, and he who is coming says: no, that is confusion and error. Give it to me! Get rid of it! It cannot be otherwise: when he comes, we must yield. If he is great, we must become small. If he lives, we must die. Why must it be? Simply because the mystery of our lives, which comes to us in him, consists in what God wants to have the world and us become, and what he wants to do with the world and with us. God loves the world. He loves it also precisely by letting it pass away before the coming of his kingdom. God's love means: I make everything new! And therefore it cannot be any other way than this: first, everything old must die.

Dying

It is appointed for mortals to die once.
(Heb. 9:27)

"End" in itself and as such means, even for Christians: thus far and no farther! You have had your time and now have no more ahead of you. You were given your chances, possibilities, and powers. They are now gone, and you can expect no more. Now nothing, absolutely nothing, can be done different, better, or again. "You must be gone; your clock has run down!" (Schiller, *Wilhelm Tell*). Was everything just a run-up—and what an arduous and troublesome run-up, both internally and externally—and, more closely examined, perhaps one single false start? Is that really supposed to be all? As far as the individual is concerned, is it finally too late for anything else? Yet now, because Christians can hope, it is not an "end in itself." No skeletal figure representing death will triumphantly hold up an hourglass with the sand run out and irrevocably put an end to the Christian. Rather, the one in whom Christians were able to believe and to love and to bear testimony to during this, their time, this very one will—when it is time, according to his gracious planning and disposition—say to them, "Stop! It's enough now. Nothing more is expected of you." How could the conclusion of Christian existence that is expected from Christ come too soon? Because it comes from him, it can only be an event that is gracious and therefore clearly to be welcomed.

Ancestors

"To him all of them are alive."
(Luke 20:38)

It is not just those currently living who have a part in the one "communion of the saints," but also the dead, and not just those who are currently alive speak and act, but with them also those who have passed on. Their words, their works, and their history are by no means finished with their departure, but often enough they do not enter into their decisive phase, which has an unbreakable connection with contemporary history, until long after their departure and in the midst of their descendants. Here there is mutual bearing and being borne, asking and being asked, and mutual responsibility among the sinners gathered there in Christ. In the church there is no past. "To him all of them are alive." One who has really passed away, who has absolutely nothing more to say, could only be an arch heretic, who is totally lost, even for the invisible church of God. There are only relative heretics, and therefore even those who have from time to time been judged as such may and should speak in their acknowledged madness. God is the Lord of the church. We cannot anticipate which coworkers of the past are welcome in our own work and which are not. It can always be that among them we will have a quite unexpected and special need for these voices that were initially very unwelcome. History wants to bear witness to the truth of God, not to our accomplishments, and therefore, again and again, we must draw back from all our presumed wonderful knowledge regarding God's truth and be prepared to learn something new.

We Will See

The Death of Death

"Where, O death, is your sting?"
(1 Cor. 15:55)

What is death next to God? If death is our last enemy, it is still not within his power to do to us what he wants to do and can do to us. God appointed him, but God can also depose him. God armed him, but God can also disarm him. So, in death we will not be alone with death; we will not be in the kingdom of a second god. Rather, with death the Lord of death will also be on the scene. We will fall into his hands and not into other hands. What we have to fear is not death but God. But even God we cannot fear without knowing that we—as inconsolable as we are otherwise—are comforted by God himself. Yet what does that mean, then, except that in the middle of death God is our Helper and Savior? The unavoidable, bitter, frightening work of death will happen to us. But for us God will be the fulfillment of all good things, even as this happens to us. So, in any case, what cannot happen to us in death is that we stop being under God's lordship, stop being his property and the objects of his love. Being able to change anything about that is also beyond the power of death. Our death is our limit, but our God is also the limit of our death. Death can take everything from us, but he cannot make it so that God is not God, our Helper and Savior and as such our hope. That death cannot do. And since he cannot do that, we must seriously ask: can he do anything at all?

Disciplined Hope

Thy kingdom come.
(Matt. 6:10, KJV)

Where the church is, there is one goal: the kingdom of God. How could it be that this goal does not cause a lasting restlessness for the people in the church whose actions bear no relationship to the greatness of this goal? We must not let it happen that in this way we cause Christian existence to be spoiled. It may well be that one would like to let the hand laid on the plow fall again, if one compares the church with its goal. Those who do not know this oppressive feeling have not yet seen the real dynamic of this matter. In the church one can only be like a bird in a cage that repeatedly slams against the bars. A whole lot more is at stake than our little bit of preaching and liturgy! Where the apostolic church is alive, however, the people know about this longing, but they do not burn out. If we really hope for the kingdom of God, then we will not be ashamed to find in this particular congregation the one holy and universal church. The Christian hope is the most revolutionary thing that one can imagine, and next to it all other revolutions are only blank cartridges. But it is a disciplined hope; it puts people in their place. Where they can be quite restless and at the same time quite peaceful, where they can be with the others in the congregation in which the members recognize each other in longing and in humility in the light of the divine humor, there they will do what has to be done. In this way the church moves with patience and with haste toward the future of the Lord.

More Restless than the Most Restless

We will see him as he is.
(1 John 3:2)

"We wait for you, O Son of God." It is the final and universal revelation of Jesus Christ as the One who he is: the One in whom God has loved and reconciled the world with himself, already established his justice for all people, already borne all their sins away, already removed all suffering, already dried all tears, already stilled all crying out, already created a new heaven and a new earth, and already brought new people onto the scene. Christians now already believe and love him as this One. But as this One he is still hidden to the world and to them, for even they do not yet know him "face to face." They are only just approaching his revelation, as well as the revelation of their own being as his brothers and sisters and as the saved and liberated children of God. They have eternal life in this revelation, but still only in the form of a promise given to them by him, not in the form of its fulfillment. What all in the church look forward to from the standpoint of the resurrection of Jesus is the fulfillment of the will of God that all people will be saved and will come to the knowledge of the truth. More restless than the most restless and more urgent than the most zealous hothead in the area, they ask, "Where are you, comfort of the whole world?"—more restless and more urgent because they are certain of this future comfort, because they are looking and moving toward the future to be fulfilled by God.

Anticipation

Rejoice.
(Phil. 4:4)

Those who would want to seal themselves off from joy would certainly not be obedient people. For they should want to be happy. People have joy in their life when they experience a large or even a small fulfillment of their wishes. Their life has reached a point at which, for the time being, it no longer takes any effort and merely offers itself as a gift. Life laughs at us, and indeed in such a way that, for the time being, we may also laugh. Real joy comes like the Holy Spirit, and it is really the Holy Spirit that comes each time when real joy comes: it comes, and no one knows from whence it comes. When we rejoice, then for us time stands still for a moment. As long as we rejoice, we would like only for the joyful moment to last. That happens, of course, only in the single case of joy in what the Holy Scripture calls eternal joy and bliss in complete communion with God. This one case, however, is exemplary for everything that is called joy. "I rejoice" means, as a rule, "I am looking forward to something." Joy, as a rule, is anticipation. Even in the experience of fulfillment itself, it is usually transformed into the anticipation of further fulfillment. Everything that we know and experience as joy here and now is interim fulfillment. In all interim forms, the will to joy must be the will to that eternal joy that is the final revelation of the fulfillment of life accomplished for us and given to us by God.

Reflection

We cannot fail to notice that God is glorious in such a way that he radiates joy, and thus everything that he is, he is in beauty. Where one says it differently, there the proclamation of his glory always has about it something that is dangerously lacking in joy, brilliance, and humor—if not to say, boring. God gives himself to his creatures. That is his glory revealed in Jesus Christ. And the creatures to whom God gives himself may praise him. Where there is light, there is an illumination. Where there is radiance, there is reflection. All creatures are to be seen from the standpoint that they have their destiny in giving in time and temporality an inappropriate but faithful response to the jubilation with which the Godhead is filled from eternity to eternity. The angels do it, but so do the lowest creatures— to our shame and for our instruction. And if human beings received their destiny again in Jesus Christ in the promise of their participation in God's glory, then they would come only as abashed latecomers into the choir of heavenly and earthly creation, whose jubilation has never been interrupted and who have always suffered and sighed only because of the failure of human beings, in incomprehensible madness and ingratitude, to join with their own voices in the jubilation surrounding them.

Nothing Will Be Lost

For all of us must appear before the judgment seat of Christ.

(2 Cor. 5:10)

I am much less interested in the punishment of this "outsider" than in the punishment that waits for me. And it consists certainly in the contrast that will become evident: on the one hand, the reality of salvation and of life, and, on the other, how little use we have made of them, and how shamefully small our gratitude has been. It is always healthiest for people to think first of all about themselves and from that standpoint to measure what it would mean if God's mercy is given to this whole ungrateful humanity and Christendom: the great nevertheless of God! For that will be judgment: the nevertheless of our gracious God. There we will be with our ocean of ingratitude, and God will say: I have loved you! And then we will all be ashamed. That will then really be eternal punishment, that we must be so ashamed, but it will be shame in the light of the abundant wealth of God's grace. That means that only then will our eyes—and those of atheists and everyone—be opened as to how much reason we have to be thankful. To see the mercy of God from eternity to eternity is more than we can take in. I have not yet looked behind the curtain, but I can conceive of it in no other way than that everything and everyone that has every been—including even theological history, which will perhaps be one of the darkest corners to be illuminated, and including the whole of natural history with all these sunken forests and all these little animals that once lived—all of that will be there. Nothing will be lost: nothing at all.

Longing

Come, Lord Jesus!
(Rev. 22:20)

Show yourself everywhere as the Lord of the godly and the ungodly, the wise and the foolish, the healthy and the sick; as the Lord also of our poor church and of all others; as the Lord of good and bad governments, and of nourished and undernourished peoples; as the Lord also of people who believe that they must say and write so much that is good and not so good; as our Lord and Protector that we may commend ourselves to your care, but also as the supreme Judge of us all, to whom we will be responsible on judgment day and even today.

Great, holy, and merciful God, we long for your final revelation, in which it will become clear to all that the whole created world and its history, as well as all people and their life histories, were, are, and will be in your loving and strict hands. We thank you that we may look forward to this revelation.

All of this we pray in the name of Jesus Christ, in which you have loved, elected, and called us human beings from eternity. Amen.

Sources

The texts of Karl Barth gathered here are selected from his extensive total works and are printed here mostly in abbreviated form. The original texts can be read in unabbreviated form and in their original contexts and in the following places.

Page	Source
3	*Einführung in die evangelische Theologie* (Zurich: EVZ Verlag, 1962), 72–74.
4	*Die Verheißung: Lukas 1* (Munich: Kaiser, 1960), 56.
5	*Predigten 1954–67* (Zurich: Theologischer Verlag, 1979), 43.
6	*Ethik II 1928/29* (Zurich:Theologischer Verlag, 1978), 444–46.
7	*Predigten 1921–35* (Zurich:Theologischer Verlag, 1998), 355–56.
8	*Predigten 1935–52* (Zurich:Theologischer Verlag, 1996), 150–51.
9	Ibid., 151–52.
10	*Die Kirchliche Dogmatik (=KD)* (Zurich: Zollikon, 1940–), II/1:727.
11	*Predigten 1921–35*, 354.
12	*Der Götze wackelt* (Berlin: Vogt, 1961), 159–61.
13	*Verheißung*, 56–57.

14   *Predigten 1935–52*, 281–82.

17   *Predigten 1917* (Zurich: Theologischer Verlag, 1999), 276–78.

18   *Dogmatik im Grundriß* (1947; 4th ed., Zurich: Theologischer Verlag, 1977), 40–46.

19   Ibid., 53–56.

20   *KD* II/2: 32–33.

21   *KD* III/3: 246–47.

22   "Die Menschlichkeit Gottes," *Theol. Stud.* 48 (1956): 14–15.

23   "Die Menschlichkeit Jesu," in *Mensch und Menschlichkeit* (Kröners Taschenbücher 243; Stuttgart: Alfred Kröner Verlag, 1956), 115ff., 120–21.

27   *Predigten 1954–67*, 236.

28   Ibid., 134–36.

29   Ibid., 190–92.

30   Ibid., 254, 256–57.

31   *KD* IV/3: 321, 403–4, 418–19.

32   *Predigten 1954–67*, 157.

33   *KD* II/2: 650–51.

37   *KD* III/1: 160, 170.

38   Ibid., 188–89.

39   Ibid., 198–99.

40   *KD* III/4: 384–88.

41   *KD* III/2: 390, 344, 347; III/4: 186–87.

42   *KD* III/4: 205, 209, 213–15.

43   Ibid., 313–14, 319.

44   Ibid., 702–4.

45   Ibid., 705–6.

46   Ibid., 708–9.

49   *Predigten 1954–67*, 234.

50   *KD* IV/1: 464, 459–60, 469, 484–85.

51   Ibid., 465, 483–84.

52   *Das christliche Leben* (Zurich: Theologischer Verlag, 1976), 363–66, 368, 378, 382, 372–73.

53   *KD* IV/2: 473–74, 489, 497–99.

54   *KD* III/4: 450–51.

55   Ibid., 614–26.

56   *KD* IV/2: 462, 465.

57   *KD* IV/3: 500–506, 432, 522.

58   *KD* III/2: 311–12.

59   *KD* III/4: 417–19, 423, 425–26.

60   *Predigten 1954–67*, 232–33.

63   Ibid., 102.

64   *Gottes Gnadenwahl*, Theologische Existenz heute 47 (Munich: Kaiser, 1936), 56.

65   *Einführung*, 112–13, 115–18.

66   "Der christliche Standpunkt," in *Unterwegs* 2 (1948): 1.

67   *KD* IV/2: 605–17.

68   *Predigten 1954–67*, 263–64.

69   *KD* III/3: 283–84.

70   Ibid., 275–76.

71   *Predigten 1954–67*, 239–40.

72   *KD* IV/2: 891–95.

73   Ibid., 718–19, 794; IV/1: 839.

77   *KD* III/4: 464–65.

78   *KD* III/2: 642.

79   *KD* III/3: 96–97.

80   *Das christliche Leben*, 462–66.

81   "Freiheit," in *Freiheit, Polis* 7 (Zurich, 1960), 2–4.

82   *KD* III/2: 270–72, 290.

83   *KD* III/4: 330–31.

84   *KD* III/2: 299–301.

85   Ibid., 302–3, 310–11.

89   *KD* IV/2: 690.

90   *Gespräche 1959–1962* (Zurich: Theologischer Verlag, 1995), 352, 354.

91   *KD* IV/3: 872–74, 884–87, 890–91, 1022.

92   *Christengemeinde und Bürgergemeinde* (Stuttgart, 1946), 11–13, 25–26.

93   *Eine Schweizer Stimme 1938–1945* (Zurich: Zollikon, 1945), 73–74, 76.

94   Ibid., 327–29.

95   *KD* III/4: 524–25.

96   *Predigten 1954–67*, 215–17.

97   *Karl Barth–Emil Brunner: Briefwechsel 1916–1966* (Zurich: Theologischer Verlag, 2000), 358.

98   *Texte zur Barmer Theologicschen Erklärung* (Zurich: Theologischer Verlag, 1984), 198, 190, 201–2, 199–200.

101   *KD* II/1: 457–72.

102   *KD* III/4: 58, 78.

103   Ibid., 602–3, 632–35.

104   *Letzte Zeugnisse* (Zurich: EVZ Verlag, 1969), 63–64.

105   *KD* IV/2: 693–94.

106   *Einführung*, 123–24, 139; *KD* IV/3: 1036–37, 1039, 1053–54.

107   *Fürchte dich nicht!* 303–4.

108   *KD* IV/3: 1063–65.

109   *KD* IV/1: 747; *Die protestantische Theologie im 19. Jh.* (Zurich: Zollikon, 1947), 3, 8.

113   *KD* III/2: 740–41, 743–44.

114   *Dogmatik im Grundriß*, 172–73.

115   *KD* IV/4 (fragment): 217–19, 221.

116   *KD* III/4: 427–31, 438–39.

117   *KD* II/1: 739, 757, 730–31.

118   Based on Eberhard Busch, *Humane Theologie: Texte und Erläuterungen zur Theologie des alten Karl Barth* (Zurich: EVZ Verlag, 1967), 31–33.

119   *Gebete* (Munich: Kaiser, 1963), 80–81.